BEYOND TOMORROW,

A Rational Utopia

by

Burnham P. Beckwith, Ph.D.

Published by B. P. Beckwith
656 Lytton Ave. (C430), Palo Alto, CA, 94301
Price:—$9.00 postpaid

CONTENTS

CHAPTER I

AWAKENING

I awoke slowly from a long deep sleep. I felt pleasantly drowsy at first. I did not open my eyes immediately because I wanted to remember the dream which had just preceeded my awakening. I had been walking through a green mountain meadow in the high Sierras, a meadow like one of those I had often hiked through in my youth. The path meandered along beside a small mountain stream. I had stopped to look at the rainbow trout and had lain down in the grass so that I could watch the trout from the stream bank without being clearly visible to them. After I had lain there quietly for a few minutes, the fish began to swim lazily by, as if on parade. Suddenly the biggest fish of all came into view. He broke water for a minute to catch an insect, and the sun glinted on his shiny scales. Even after he submerged, the light reflected from his scales grew stronger and stronger. It began to dazzle my eyes, and all at once I woke up.

When I opened my eyes, I saw a light directly above me. The turning on of this light must have awakened me.

I did not know where I was. I was lying on my back in what looked like a hospital bed in a hospital room with light green walls and a white glass ceiling. But I could not remember how or when I had gotten there. In fact I could remember nothing of my past except the dream.

I tried to move but found that I was securely but comfortably bound to the bed, which had a metal grille on each side, so that I could not fall out. I looked around the room and saw a door at one end, on the right, and a large, curtained window at the left end. It was dark outside. Then, turning my neck a little more to the left, I detected a nurse standing beside the head of my bed. This effort made me feel weak and dizzy.

Observing my movement, the nurse spoke to me in a language I could not understand.

I tried to speak to her but found I was incapable of speech.

Then the bright light overhead went out, and the ceiling became a dim pastel pink which very

slowly turned to red and then to green, then to a
sea of undulating rainbows, and so on in cycles.
This symphony of color was accompanied by soft
background music, which occasionally reminded me of
the sound of a mountain stream. Hence my dream of
such a stream and rainbow trout. Like most dreams,
it needed no Freudian explanation. I soon fell
asleep again.

1. Where Am I?

When I awoke and opened my eyes again, it was
daylight, and the color symphony and background
music had ended. Several extraordinarily handsome
but curiously dressed adults stood around my bed.
I had heard them talking among themselves in an
unknown but musical tongue as I gradually became
conscious. When I first opened my eyes, they
muttered a few exclamations and suddenly became
quiet. As my mind cleared, I glanced from one to
the other questioningly.

On my left was the young nurse I had observed
on my previous awakening. I now realized suddenly,
with an almost electric shock, that she was the most
beautiful woman I had ever seen close up. She wore
a chic nurse's hat and a light green uniform, marked
with the pink letters, DD, just above her swelling
bosom. Suddenly, she smiled charmingly, and I found
it hard to shift my gaze to the other persons present.

Two incredibly handsome men, one young and one
middle-aged, both in curious green coveralls, stood
at the foot of the bed. On my right stood a strik-
ing, middle-aged woman, in a light pink pant suit.

No one spoke, but all looked interested.
After some struggle with my tongue and mouth I
was finally able to ask, "Where am I?"

The older woman answered in heavily accented
English, "You are in the Los Angeles General Hospital. You have been unconscious for a long time.
You will recover soon, but now you must rest as much
as possible."

As she finished speaking, all the other observers turned and filed silently out of the room.
Only the friendly handsome older lady remained.
After a moment she said, "My name is Bee Four. I am
a special nurse. What is your name?"

I started to tell her my name, but suddenly
realized I could not recall it. Then, as I puzzled
over my name, I became aware that I had no memory of

the past.

"I don't know," I replied, "and what's more I don't seem to remember anything."

"That's natural," she said. "Don't worry about it. Your memory will return as you recover."

There were many questions I wanted to ask her but I felt terribly tired and weak. I closed my eyes and rested for a few minutes. Then I heard some one entering my room. I opened my eyes and saw my beautiful young nurse carrying a bowl of some liquid and a glass tube. She sat on a chair beside my bed, put one end of the curved glass tube in the bowl, and the other end near my mouth. My older guide said, "That is a liquid food which should not upset your stomach."

The pretty nurse smiled fetchingly and said, "Too too."

I accepted the tube in my mouth and sucked in a mouthful of the food. It tasted so good I had no trouble in finishing the bowl. Then I was given some red and green pills.

"I'd like another bowl," I said, "I didn't realize how hungry and thirsty I was."

"She will bring you another bowl in two hours," Bee Four said. "You mustn't eat too much too soon. It might upset your stomach."

A feeling of pleasant warmth spread through my body. I closed my eyes and dozed off. It seemed only a moment until I felt a tap on my shoulder, opened my eyes, and saw the young nurse with another bowl of soup and more pills beside me. I drank, dozed off again, and woke once more to a tap on the shoulder. So passed the rest of my first, partly conscious, day in that hospital.

When I awoke on the second day I felt more alert and more hungry. I turned my head and saw Bee Four sitting in a rocking chair by the window. I noticed that there were no traffic noises of any kind, and that the sky outside seemed free of smog.

Bee Four saw my movement and asked me how I felt.

"I feel much better," I said. "Why is it so quiet outside, and what happened to the smog?"

"Smog," she answered, "What is smog?"

She must be one of those foreign nurses, I thought. I remembered that American hospitals had been hiring many foreign doctors and nurses because we had failed to train enough to provide for our needs. Suddenly I realized that my memory was re-covering in small pieces.

"What country do you come from?" I asked.

"I was born and raised here in Los Angeles," she replied. "Where do you come from?"

Again I searched my mind, but could find no definite answer. I felt that I too was a native of the city, but could remember no details.

At this moment my beautiful blonde nurse came through my door again with another bowl of soup. It proved to be thicker and more satisfying than before.

After a post-breakfast nap, I was awakened for a medical examination. The tall handsome older doctor who examined me had been one of my observers when I awoke the day before. He used some equipment I had never seen. He was non-communicative. To start a conversation, I asked him to explain why the hospital personnel were all so handsome. He looked puzzled, and turned towards Bee Four with a question on his face. She spoke a few foreign words and he smiled. She said to me:

"We will answer that and other questions when you have recovered."

After the medical examination, I dozed off again, and spent the rest of the day sleeping and resting between feedings by my beauty queen. Each time I saw her, I fell more in love with her.

Several more days passed in this restful and pleasant way, with frequent color symphonies and much soft background music. On the fourth day I sat up in bed. On the fifth day I took some steps around the room. I looked out the window but I could see nothing but trees, and the sky. On the sixth day I began going to the adjoining bath room on my own. And all the time my memory was improving. First I remembered my name, John Taylor Putnam. Then I began to recall my childhood in Pasadena, then my college days at Harvard, then my brief career as a professor at Stanford, my married life, and so on. I told Bee Four about these experiences as I recalled them, but she was very reticent about her own. I gathered that she had been a professor of languages and that she was a volunteer aid in the hospital. I could not understand why she spent so much of her time with me. It seemed inconceivable that she alone spoke English in an American hospital but I was still too confused and vague about my own past to question her sharply about her own.

On my seventh conscious day in the hospital I asked for some different music and Bee Four placed a radio on the table beside my bed. I could receive

-4-

many different unfamiliar musical programs, but
nothing else. I noted that there were no commercials, and that the program notes were in a language
I could not understand. On my ninth day I asked for
some reading matter. Bee Four asked me what authors
I preferred, and I mentioned Rex Stout and C. P.
Snow. The next morning she brought me a dozen
novels by Stout, Snow, and other authors. The paper
and the binding were of a sort I had never seen, and
the prefaces and copyright pages had been cut out.
I asked for a TV set, but she said the doctor feared
that TV programs would overstimulate me. I wondered
why I was being treated in this way.

I had repeatedly asked Bee Four why I was in
the hospital, why the doctor and the nurses did not
talk to me, and other related questions, but she
always answered that it would be better for me to
recall what had happened. I began to suspect that I
was in a hospital or hospital wing for the mentally
ill. On the seventh day, when returning from my
private bathroom to my bed, I observed that Bee Four
was looking out the window, and I made a slight
detour to try my room door to the hall. It was
locked, as I had feared. When I asked Bee Four the
reason, she said it was for my protection.

I awoke during the following night, and lay
awake trying to decide if I was out of my mind and
really needed to be confined. After a while I recalled that I had once read that only sane people
question their own sanity. This thought encouraged
me, although I had always been skeptical of the
theory. So many popular truths are really false-
hoods.

I began to ask myself what I could have done to
make people think I was insane. I considered the
possibility of a violent attack on some other person, but this seemed unlikely because I could recall
no acts of or temptation to violence. Nor could I
recall any violence by my parents or relatives. I
next considered drug addiction and alcoholism, but I
could remember no such illness in my own or my
relatives' experience. Then I began to consider
depression, a common cause or symptom of mental illness. I asked myself if I had experienced, recently,
some seriously depressing experience. This query
seemed to ring a bell. Suddenly my wife's death,
and then my doctor's prognosis of terminal cancer of
the lungs came to mind. A few more moments of concentration and I remembered my decision to be frozen
alive.

I had always been fascinated by stories about
the rapid advance of science, especially by stories
about efforts to preserve life indefinitely by sudden
deep freezing. When my doctor had advised me that
my cancer was incurable, I had decided to have my
body frozen and preserved until cancer could be
cured. As a wealthy man without any remaining family, I had found it easy to make the necessary
arrangements. I had delivered myself to the Los
Angeles Cryogenic Laboratory on July 10, 1982, had
been put to sleep, and then, I assumed, deep frozen.
But something must have gone wrong. And apparently
I had been placed in an institution for the mentally
sick to prevent any more suicidal attempts. This
conclusion explained many, but not all, the odd
features of my hospital experience. I decided to
sleep again and resume my analytical meditation in
the morning. My mind had become clearer, and I was
determined to ask more critical and more searching
questions on the morrow.

The next morning, after I had had my breakfast—
now a very solid affair, but consisting of odd-tast-
ing foods—and after I had received my daily examination from the handsome but silent doctor, I informed Bee Four of the further progress in the recovery
of my memory. She smiled and complimented me on my
progress.

"You will soon be as well as ever," she said.

"How can I be as well as ever when I am dying
of cancer?" I asked.

"You will not die of cancer," she replied, with
great assurance. "The green pills you have been
taking daily have already arrested and will soon
cure your cancer."

This astonishing and completely unexpected
reply gave me pause for some minutes. I must be in
the hands of quacks, I thought, for I was well aware
that no orthodox, respectable doctor claimed to be
able to cure lung cancer with pills. However, I had
known that large sums were being spent on research
and that many new cancer-killing drugs were being
tested. Perhaps I am in a research program testing
new drugs, I thought, or perhaps Bee Four is a
Christian Scientist.

I decided to attack on a different front.

"Why is the door to my room locked?" I asked.

"It's locked to keep curious people out," she
replied. "You are an object of wide general interest, and we do not wish visitors and reporters to
interfere with your recovery."

This sounded fairly plausible. I knew that reporters often annoyed and embarrassed persons
accused of crime. Suicide was still a crime, and the
manner of my suicidal effort had certainly been
newsworthy.

"Why are you the only person I have met here who
speaks English, and why do you speak it with an
accent," I asked.

"I can see you are recovering your mental capacity. I will report your progress to your medical
committee. Soon they will allow me to answer all
your questions."

When Bee Four entered my room the next morning,
she told me that she had reported my recovery of
memory to my medical committee and that they had
authorized an important change in my treatment. She
said she would discuss it with me after my morning
medical examination.

I was so curious I could hardly wait to finish
my breakfast and my medical exam. When the time came
for her report, I noticed that the doctor and the
nurse both remained close to my bed. Bee Four pulled
her chair up beside my bed and smiled at me encouragingly.

"What do you think happened to you after your
suicide attempt?" she asked.

"That's fairly obvious," I replied, "my effort
must have been frustrated. Perhaps the police learned of my efforts and intervened. Perhaps the manager
of the Cryogenic Institute got cold feet and changed
his mind after the freezing process had injured but
had not frozen me. The only thing I can't understand
is why you have been unwilling to tell me what happened."

2. The Incredible Answer

"I can now tell you all you want to know," said
Bee Four. "But you must be prepared for what may be
a great shock." She paused for a long moment and
smiled encouragingly. "Your plan was not frustrated.
Almost 500 years have passed since your body was frozen alive."

Here she paused and observed me carefully but
warmly. The nurse and the doctor also studied my
face.

"This is no time for joking," I said. "Please
be serious."

I turned to look at the doctor and the nurse.
Both were watching me very thoughtfully. Clearly

they were not amused, but then I remembered that
perhaps they could not understand English.

"You have good reason to be skeptical," Bee
Four resumed. "No sensible person of your time
would accept my statement without far more evidence
than you have seen. But you have already observed
various small things that have puzzled you——the
unknown language spoken by the doctor and other persons, the odd clothes they wear, the strange equipment they use, the locked door, my accent, and so
forth. I speak English with a strange accent because I am a professor of dead languages, one of the
few in this city who can speak 20th-century English."

She paused and smiled encouragingly. The nurse
put her finger on my wrist to monitor my pulse. The
doctor put an odd looking stethescope on my heart.
All waited expectantly. I glanced from one face to
the other; then at the medical instruments, the odd
clothing, and certain curious minor features of the
room. Perhaps they were serious! And, after all,
I too had once believed in and longed for such an
experience. My heart began to beat faster and faster. I took a very deep breath, but it did not help.
My face felt warm, and then I lost consciousness.

When I again became conscious, my three observers were still watching me carefully. When I recalled what had caused me to faint, my heart began
to pound again, but this time I remained alert.

"It's fantastic, it's incredible, but I'm beginning to believe it," I said. "When can I see the
world outside?"

"You're naturally excited," Bee Four said.
"The doctor will give you a tranquilizer, and after
you have rested for an hour, I will take you to the
roof of the hospital and let you view the new city
of Los Angeles for the first time."

The doctor gave me a blue pill to swallow, the
nurse gave me a glass of water, and, after I had
taken the pill, they both left the room.

My heart gradually resumed its normal beat, but
my mind ran wild. Had I really survived, frozen,
through five centuries? If so, what had happened to
mankind during these centuries? A thousand and one
more specific questions entered my mind, one after
the other. When I began to present them to Bee
Four, she advised me that I had had enough excitement for the moment and should rest until my visit
to the hospital roof.

Finally, after minutes that seemed hours, the

young nurse returned with an electric wheel chair.
Bee Four explained its simple control mechanism, and
we started for the roof. Nothing in the corridor or
the elevator seemed incredible except the people we
passed, all of whom, even the sick, were remarkably
handsome in appearance. Of course, the hospital
equipment and fittings all seemed strange, but they
had begun to seem strange when I had visited hospitals in my earlier life, a period of rapid technological and architectural change.

3. My First View of the New City

The hospital building had four wings, and was
over 20 stories tall. When my wheel chair rolled
out onto the roof garden, dotted with potted plants
and garden furniture, I saw that I would have a fine
view of the entire city. There was an outdoor cafe
in the center of the roof, but an open recreational
area surrounded it on all sides. I proceeded directly to the nearest point from which I could look
out over half of the city.
It was a perfect spring day. There was no smog
and I could see for a great distance. I noticed at
once that there were only two other skyscrapers in
this part of town, and that they were several hundred feet apart. All the streets were curved and
lined with trees, lawns, and gardens. There were no
parking lots among the nearby buildings and I could
see no motor vehicles except a few slowly moving
buses on certain streets. The other streets seemed
to be restricted to pedestrians and bicycles. A half
a mile away there was a wide greenbelt which apparently surrounded this entire district. There were
no small buildings standing alone or next to each
other. Every building block or site was occupied
by a single large handsome, colorful building surrounded by a wide band of lawn and garden. There
were no grey or ugly buildings or walls. And every
building had a patio and garden on its roof. Each
street and neighborhood had obviously been designed
as a single harmonious, planned landscape, or rather
cityscape.
Beyond the immediate urban district in which we
were, I could see other urban districts, each largely hidden by trees and surrounded by a wide greenbelt. There were freeways running through these
greenbelts, and entering the urban districts at certain points, but I could see none within any district.

I was at last convinced that I was living in a new age. There had been talk of such planned garden cities in my day, but none had ever been consructed. And I could tell from certain geographical features that this one occupied the site of old Los Angeles. Both Mount Wilson and the Hollywood Hills were visible through the clear smogless air. I remained silent, astonished and enthralled by the incredible spectacle before me!

Up to this very moment I had been skeptical of the almost unbelievable explanation Bee Four had given me, but as I gazed at the beautiful and very real garden city before me I was suddenly convinced that her story was true. Practical jokers or experimental psychologists could easily have prepared the interior hospital settings and events I had experienced, but not even a billionaire movie producer could have created an entire garden city or abolished auto traffic and smog in Los Angeles.

As I grasped that the cityscape before me was real and tangible, a feeling of extraordinary pleasure and satisfaction swept over me. Like Columbus I had found a strange new world, but, unlike him, I knew what I had found, and how much more I would learn about it. All the many questions I had often asked about the future would now soon be answered. I felt an overpowering eagerness to satisfy my curiosity, but I knew I should proceed slowly and systematically. After many moments of silent delight, I began by telling Bee Four that I did not recognize any of the local streets or buildings. I askd her where our hospital, was located.

"This hospital is located on land that was once a part of the old University of Southern California," she informed me. "It is part of the center or nucleus of a new planned garden city on part of the site of old Los Angeles. The new city has a population of about 400,000, and occupies only a small part of the area occupied by your Los Angeles."

"What is a city nucleus?" I inquired.

"The nucleus of each planned city contains only those facilities used by all city residents—such as a large department store, a research library, a specialized hospital, an auditorium, an art museum, a stadium, a courthouse, a jail, and so forth--and residential and commercial buildings for those employed in these facilities. The great majority of the city's population live in nearby satellite towns, each providing employment, schools, stores, and recreation for nearly all its inhabitants, most

of whom walk or cycle to and from work each day.
They visit the city center or nucleus about once a
week on the average, but can reach it by bus in less
than ten minutes from the center of their town because such centers are less than four miles from the
city center."

4. City Traffic

I drove my wheel chair slowly around the circum-
ference of the roof. The air was clear in every
direction. I could even see Catalina Island beyond
San Pedro.
"How did you get rid of the smog?" I asked.
"Mostly by doing things which could easily have
been done in your time and were in fact done soon
thereafter," Bee Four replied. "We banished the
private car from city streets and required all trucks
and buses to use non-polluting motors. Now, of
course, all urban vehicles are powered by quiet electric motors, and all electricity is generated in
pollution-free nuclear-fusion plants."
"If private cars are now non-polluting, why do
you still bar them from city streets?" I asked.
"There are five major reasons," she answered.
"First, we believe that nearly all urban residents
benefit from the exercise of walking, jogging, or
cycling to work or school and back. Secondly, the
production and use of private cars used to consume
enormous quantities of irreplaceable natural resources, which have become steadily less abundant
since your time. We have found that the virtual
elimination of private motor vehicles is the easiest
and least costly method of conserving natural resources. Thirdly, the use of private motor cars in
urban areas resulted in millions of accidents, personal injuries, and deaths. We place a much higher
value on human life and health than your contemporaries did. Fourth, we discovered that the street
noise caused by auto traffic was as harmful as the
air pollution. Finally, the drastic reduction in
street traffic we have achieved has sharply cut the
cost of building and maintaining city streets and
traffic-control systems."
"But how can people who live miles from their
jobs walk, jog or cycle to work?" I protested.
"We have few cities of over half a million population," she replied, "and each city is divided into
largely self-contained towns of forty to sixty

-11-

thousand people, nearly all of whom work or attend
school in the town they live in. In other words, we
have rebuilt all old cities and constructed all new
cities in such a way that almost every employed person can walk to work in less than twenty minutes,
and can jog or cycle to work in less than ten minutes. Young children, of course, live much closer
to their schools."

    "But surely you have not abolished bad weather,"
I said. "How do people get to work when it is rain-
ing or cold winds are blowing?"

    "We have perfected special clothing which keeps
walkers, joggers, and cyclists dry and warm in the
worst weather," Bee Four replied. "Weather is rarely a serious problem in Southern California. And
most Americans now live in regions with mild climates. In colder climates, special measures have
been taken to protect walkers, joggers, and cyclers
in bad weather. There are more underground passages,
covered walks, and heated sidewalks. In all cities
the great majority of workers walk, jog, or cycle to
work throughout the year."

    By this time I was beginning to feel rather
tired, and Bee Four must have noticed, for she immediately remarked that I had surely had enough excitement for one day and should return to my bed for the
rest of the day. She guided me to the elevator, and
from there to my room, where I found my bed unusually
appealing and restful. I tried to plan and formulate
some of the many questions I wanted to ask, but soon
fell asleep and slept until lunch.

    When I awoke for lunch, I noted that a strange
clock and calendar had been placed on the wall opposite the foot of the bed. I was too hungry to ask
about it before finishing my delicious lunch, but,
immediately thereafter I asked Bee Four to explain
these odd-looking objects.

5.   The New Calendar

    "The oblong white frame at the top is an elec-
tric clock-calendar. The two top numbers in black
give the hour and minute of time. Our day has 20
hours, each hour has 50 minutes, and each minute has
50 seconds. The two lower numbers in red give the
day of the month and the month of the year, in that
order. Our year has twelve 30-day months, four
quarter-end holidays, and one or two year-end holidays. The paper calendar below the electric clock

shows a standard 30-day month and its six five-day
weeks. Every month begins on the same day of the
month, the first day of the first week, and ends on
the last day of the last week."

"Why did you change from a 24-hour day to a 20-
hour day?" I enquired.

"Because we have a 5-day week, and wanted it to
contain just 100 hours. Whenever possible we have
applied the metrical system to the calendar, for the
same reasons you had already applied it to money and
other units of measurement. Its use makes all measurement and business accounting easier. For instance, sales reports and profit-and-loss statements
are more useful when they cover the same number and
kind of days and months. Unfortunately a 365-day
year cannot be fully metricized."

"Your calendars do not show the names of the
days of the week," I objected.

"Since all weeks and months are uniform, we
have no need for non-numerical day names. We simply
refer to any day by its number in the week."

"But didn't Christians object to having their
holy seventh day turned into an ordinary work day?"
I asked.

"Yes, they did. But when the calendar reform
was adapted by the world government, less than 10%
of the world population was Christian and only a minority of them were fundamentalists. Liberal Christians did not object to the calendar reform. Moreover, for a long time, all countries allowed religious persons to keep their old religious holidays
and to make up for this by working on some other day
of the week. Nearly all our business firms now
operate every day of the week in order to reduce
capital costs per unit of output, but all workers
enjoy at least one full day off each week. Thus we
can permit conservative Christians and Jews to
celebrate their sabbath without treating them dif-
ferently from other workers, and without requiring
non-Christians to rest on the Christian sabbath."

"What is the meaning of the large number, 411,
at the top of the paper calendar page?" I asked.

"That means that this is the 411th year since
the creation of our world government," Bee Four replied. "When the new world government designed our
uniform world calendar, it had to abandon the Western custom of dating events from the birth of Christ
because the great majority of the world's population
were non-Christian, and would not accept a Christian
base for the new calendar. The calendar reformers

-13

believed that the creation of a world government able
to preserve world peace and order was the most important event in world history, and they therefore used
the date of this great event as the base for the new
world calendar. The choice was popular because all
the peoples of the world were favorably affected by
this event."

By this time I was again becoming sleepy. I
kept repeating the incredible phrase, "Year 411,
year 411, year 411" to myself until I fell asleep
again, and slept soundly until awakened for supper.
After supper I listened for a while to a musical program on the small radio Bee Four had placed on a
table beside my bed, and then fell asleep again.

CHAPTER II

MY SECOND DAY ON TOP

When I awoke the next morning, I did not at
first know where I was. I studied the room for a
moment, and realized I was obviously in a hospital.
Then I saw the calendar on the wall. It said, "411."
All at once I recalled the incredible events of
yesterday. Or had I dreamt it all? I opened and
closed my eyes, I felt the bed clothes. I pinched
myself. I stared at the calendar again. At this
moment Bee Four opened my door, entered, and greeted
me in her odd foreign accent. It was not a dream!
Incredibly, it was real! My heart began to thump,
and I was speechless for a few minutes. Before I
had recovered, my handsome young doctor entered and
began to feel my pulse. He smiled and said something to Bee Four in a foreign tongue. She inter-
preted, "The doctor says you are a little excited,
but that you have stood the strain of orientation
very well."

Soon after the doctor left, my beauteous blond
nurse entered with a breakfast tray, designed for
use as a bed table. It contained fruit, bacon, and
toast, all of a kind and quality I had never tasted
in my former life. And how hungry I was!

After I had finished my breakfast, and the
nurse had taken my tray away, I told Bee Four how
eager I was to return to the roof garden and gaze
upon the garden city around me. She brought me my
new dressing gown, socks, carpet slippers, and sun
glasses and helped me settle down in my comfortable,
well-padded, electric wheel chair. As we passed
through the hospital hall and elevator,I again marveled at the extraordinary good looks and apparent
good health of the other hospital inmates and staff.
I could only distinguish the patients from the staff
by the fact that they wore hospital clothing and
looked slightly paler and thinner, like stylish
models in my day.

As soon as we reached the edge of the roof garden, Bee Four sat down in a yellow canvas rocking
chair beside me and remained silent while I again
gazed enraptured upon the glorious cityscape before
me, a prospect which no other person of my era had
ever seen, or even imagined. For the second time I
felt like Columbus on his first sight of the new
world, or Cortes upon first viewing the Aztec
capital. How extraordinary that I should have

-15-

survived to view this incredible garden city!

I think I would have been happy to gaze upon it in silence indefinitely, but after my heart resumed its normal level and I could think clearly again, I could not help asking questions to satisfy my intense curiosity.

1. City Planning

"Why are there so few tall buildings?" I queried. "In my day every large city had many tall buildings, called skyscrapers, and futuristic architects like Soleri dreamed of, and actually planned and wrote about, megastructures a mile high."

"Yes, there were many such proposals in your century," Bee Four replied. "But they ignored the fact that every increase in building height above four or five stories increases costs per cubic foot of space, including land, street, and utility costs. The biggest cost jump occurs when elevators become necessary, but most other structural costs per unit of usable space rise as each additional floor is added. The construction of tall buildings uses up large quantitites of costly irreplaceable metals. The thoughtless waste of such resources in your age, and continued use since then, have exhausted all high-grade and middle-grade ore and petroleum deposits. Moreover, the people of Asia, Africa, and South America now have a standard of living far above that of Americans in your own day. To conserve metal, we have not only reduced by 90% the number of tall buildings in large cities but have also housed nearly all urban residents in low multi-family buildings or row houses. They permit large economies in construction. Very few of our residential buildings are tall enough to require the use of steel and/or elevators, which waste both space and metals. The tall buildings in this city center were authorized to improve our cityscape aesthetically and to reduce sharply the land area of the city center, thus enabling all town residents to live closer to it. There are also one or two tall buildings in the center of each town for similar reasons."

"But in my time," I said, "it was an axiom of real estate theory that land in the center of a large city is worth far more, often over a hundred times more, than land on the outer limits of the city. Aren't you wasting valuable city-center land by not using it more intensively, and thereby earning higher rents?"

"No, for several reasons. First, we have decentralized most of the economic activities which
used to be concentrated in city centers. Almost
every worker is now employed near his home. Hardly
anyone commutes daily into a city center. Secondly,
the elimination of competition in business has radically reduced the amount of land needed to perform
each remaining city-center function, and consequently
has drastically reduced competitive bidding for
city-center land. Finally, the relative rise in the
price of steel and other metal building components
has made intensive use of such land much less economic."
     As I resumed my exciting study of the incredible
city around us, I felt that I could never grow tired
of this scene. I was again impressed by the omni-
presence of trees, gardens, and flowers in the heart
of this new Los Angeles, and by the beauty and
colors of the buildings.
     °You must spend very large sums on architecture
and gardening," I remarked. "We could never have
afforded such luxuries."
     "I doubt that," Bee Four answered. "Our build-
ings last two or three times longer than yours.
Technological progress in housing and city planning
is now much slower than in your day. And, since our
cities do not grow, it is rarely necessary to tear
down old buildings to replace them with larger or
different ones. Hence, we can spend two or three
times as much per building on architecture and orna-
mentation without increasing total national spending
per year on these luxuries. Moreover, all approved
architectural plans are used over and over again.
They are not private property, as in your time. We
do spend far more on trees and gardens in business
districts, but the cost of the land so used is less
than 10% of the cost of such urban land in your
cities."
     "If your cities do not grow, how do you provide
housing and jobs for additional population?" I
queried.

2. Building New Cities

     "The population of North America and the world
has been declining slowly for over three hundred
years. But, in those few regions where population
is now growing because of migration, additional
population is housed in new cities. Each existing
city was built or rebuilt to house a certain ideal

population, and the steady rise in the standard of
living since it was constructed has made necessary a
steady reduction of its population in order to provide more spacious housing and recreational areas
for the population without encroaching on its greenbelts. Each new city is planned so as to facilitate
the continuous reconstruction which will be needed
to house fewer people more luxuriously in a given
city area."

"Do you mean to imply that each new city is
planned and built as a single construction project
before anyone moves into it?" I asked.

"Yes indeed," she replied. "This simplifies
planning and reduces both the cost of construction
and the discomfort to residents caused by reconstruction in occupied cities. It is far cheaper per
unit to construct 100,000 dwellings at a time on
vacant land than to build individual houses on
scattered lots in existing cities. There were large-
scale builders in your day who could achieve some of
the economies of mass housing construction, but none
of them could assure jobs for all tenants and
achieve immediate 100% occupancy of all new housing.
Your large builders wasted on selling and vacancy
costs much of the money they saved by pioneering
large-scale housing construction. Our city builders
build schools, stores, clinics, and public utilities,
as well as housing, at the same time, and they have
selling, repossession, and vacancy costs less than
20% of those experienced by your builders."

"But how can your city builders assure jobs
for all new residents?"

"Because every industry is organized as a giant
national monopoly, and because the government has
stabilized the growth of total demand. This makes
it possible for each monopoly to predict its sales
of each product for many years ahead. When it auth-
orizes the construction of a new plant in a new town
it can be sure that the new plant will be able to
sell its planned output and provide permanent employment for its workers. The investment plans of
different monopolies are co-ordinated by a national
investment co-ordination committee, which enables
the national construction trust to provide new major
export plants and offices for all new cities. Of
course, as I explained before, we build few new
cities now because our population is declining. But
in the twenty-first century over a hundred large new
cities were built in the United States, mostly along
the Pacific and Gulf Coasts."

3. City Government

"Which of these handsome buildings is your city hall?" I inquired.

"We have no city hall because we have no city or other local governments," Bee Four replied.

I was so taken aback by this unexpected answer that I had to remain silent for a moment to phrase a reasonable protest.

"If you have no city government," I countered, "who solves local social problems? For instance, who repairs streets, enforces criminal laws, and puts out fires?"

"All such local functions are performed by local units of national agencies. Thus, local police and firemen are employed and controlled by the National Crime and Fire Prevention Agency. Incidentally, all police are trained to work as firemen also, and vice versa, which makes them much more productive. City streets are maintained by local employees of the National Utilities Trust because these workers often dig up city streets in order to maintain and improve local utility services, and can use the same equipment for both kinds of maintenance work."

"But surely local residents should control such local services," I objected. "Only local residents are directly affected by such services and are aware of how well or badly they are performed."

"If that is true," Bee Four countered, "why did you allow telephone services, postal services, insurance, and many other local services to be performed by national or regional agencies?"

This reasonable question made me stop and think for a minute or so, before admitting, "I really cannot answer that question, except to suggest that custom determined the functions of local governments in my day."

"City governments first appeared and developed at a time when national governments were both weak and remote," Bee Four explained. "As national governments grew stronger and more sophisticated, and as the means of transport and communication improved, the need for local government steadily diminished. It had virtually ended in your time, and the survival of local government was already largely a result of cultural lag, a fact of which many social scientists were aware. As a result, the social services of national governments were already expanding rapidly.

By the year 2100 (your calendar) nearly all former local government services had been fully transfered to national governments in the most advanced nations."

4. City-Center Planning

I noticed a small residential neighborhood on one side of the hospital, about in the center of the city center, and asked Bee Four who lived there. She said it housed all workers employed in the hospital and other city-center facilities.

"The basic principle of our city planning," she continued, "is that all workers should live near their jobs. Since the city center has no large factory or other major export plant, it employs relatively few workers and has only one residential village. The surrounding towns all have many more residents and several such villages."

"Surely some families must have members who are employed in two or more separate communities," I objected.

"Very few," she replied. "The city center offers a very wide variety of jobs, as does each town within the city, and local residents are favored for local jobs. Those few families who have one member employed in the city center and one in some adjacent town are required to live in the town because we wish to keep the city center as small as possible."

"Why do you wish to keep it small?" I asked.

"Because every increase in its area increases the distance which every town resident must travel to reach the center of the city center, and also increases the average distance which a city-center resident must travel to reach the nearest greenbelt. An increase in the size of a town only affects the residents of that town, i.e., usually less than 15% of the total city population, but an increase in the size of the city center affects all city residents."

"I can see no evidence of a subway, railroad, or streetcar system," I remarked. "How do your town residents travel to and from the city center?"

"Most travel by electric buses, although many cycle to and from the city center. Since few town residents work in the city center, the average town resident visits the city less than once a week, and the entire city has only some 400,000 residents As a result, the volume of traffic is much too small to justify a subway. We have found that electric buses are the most economical method of handling the

reduced volume of passenger traffic. No railroad
line is permitted in any city."

"But surely you need railroads to deliver heavy
freight to factories and wholesalers in the city,"
I protested.

"All our railroad lines run between, not within,
cities. Each city has a railroad freight station
and a wholesale warehouse just outside its outer
greenbelt. Freight deliveries to buyers within the
city are made by electric trucks, which run mostly on
greenbelt freeways and rarely pass through residential areas. When these freeways enter built-up city
or town areas, they are depressed or covered over so
that little traffic noise escapes, and all local
streets and paths can cross them at ground level."

5. Regional Planning

"In my time the Los Angeles metropolitan area
occupied over 2000 square miles," I remarked. "How
large is it now?"

"The size of the city around you, Los Angeles
proper, is now less than 80 square miles, including
the outer recreational greenbelt areas. The city
consists of a round city center or nucleus about two
miles in diameter, and a ring of eight pear-shaped
satellite towns, each about two miles long. The
outer recreational and transport greenbelt averages
about a mile in width."

"If Los Angeles now occupies less than 80 square
miles, how do you use the other 1900 square miles the
metropolitan area once included?" I asked.

"It is occupied by intercity greenbelts and by
other planned garden cities of about the same size
and shape. Pasadena, Glendale, Santa Monica, and
Long Beach still exist and are all about the same
size as Los Angeles. There are no farms in the Los
Angeles Basin or in other valleys near the ocean.
The intercity areas consist entirely of parks and
greenbelts used for recreational activities and
facilities—hiking, picnicing, golf, archery, bird
watching, watersports on artificial lakes, zoos,
botanical gardens, etc. Agriculture is restricted to
less desirable climatic areas."

"What is the total population of California
now?" I queried.

"Your California no longer exists. But the area
included in old California now has a population of
over 80,000,000. It includes most of the finest
climatic zones in North America, and Americans today

are able to live where the climate is best. They no
longer need to live on a river or near natural resources. Hence, the great majority of them live
along the Pacific Coast, the Gulf Coast, and the
South Atlantic Coast. The old California coast is
by far the most densely populated. We require at
least five miles of greenbelt between all inland
cities, but along most of the California coast this
requirement has been sharply reduced in order to
permit more people to enjoy the very fine climate
near the ocean. Moreover, much of this coast has
been terraced and extended into the ocean in order to
provide more urban residential space."

"But how can so many people live in a semi-arid
region where water supplies were already inadequate
in my day?" I asked.

"We now get all the fresh water we need for most
coastal cities from the nearby ocean. We have giant
nuclear-fusion power stations which take the salt and
other valuable minerals out of sea water. The sale
of the salt and other minerals covers nearly all of
the desalting costs. Most of our gold, silver,
copper, nickel, and other nonferrous metals are now
extracted from sea water."

6. Eugenics

When I finally ceased gazing with wonder at the
marvelous garden city around the hospital, I began to
notice the people strolling and sitting around me on
the hospital roof garden. They were all dressed in
colorful costumes and looked incredibly strong, handsome, and good-natured. Nearly all the nurses looked
as beautiful and charming as my own DD.

Turning to Bee Four, I asked, "If this is a hospital, how is it that everyone here looks so healthy
and handsome?"

"That is largely the result of over 400 years of
eugenic policies," she replied. "Most of these
patients look weak or ill to us, but our weak and ill
must look strong and healthy to anyone reared in your
century. Of course, better nutrition, education,
family care, and medical care have helped to improve
mankind, but we estimate that 80% of the improvement
you refer to is due to eugenic measures."

"And what were these eugenic measures?" I asked.

"By far the most important has been the long-
continuing use of artificial insemination. This
practice had already begun in your day, and during
the next century the governments of all advanced

countries began to subsidize and rationalize the practice. By the year 2050, any American couple that desired to have superior children could have the wife inseminated with almost any desired type of sperm at government expense. Since parents are naturally eager to have children who will succeed in life, and since the children of those parents who first used artificial insemination achieved far greater success- es in every field of activity than most other child- ren, the number of parents who voluntarily chose to use artificial insemination grew steadily. By 2150 A.D. the vast majority of all children in advanced countries were the result of artificial insemination with sperm obtained from handsome, healthy, long- lived, emotionally stable, high I.Q. males. Their nominal fathers had voluntarily chosen sterilization long before marriage as the cheapest and most effect- ive method of birth control."

"In my day," I observed, "most fathers wanted to believe that their children were of their own blood, as we mistakenly phrased it, and looked like them, or like some member of their family. How were their attitudes changed?"

"In several ways, first by explaining that par- ents of adopted children were as fond of their child- ren as were parents of natural children. Secondly, by creating diversified semen banks which made it possible for parents to choose the type of children— blond or brunette, tall or short, etc.—which would result from artificial insemination. Thirdly, by spreading the growing knowledge about the many defec- tive genes carried by most males and about the her- editary causes of most illness and unhappiness. The science of genetics advanced very rapidly from 1950 to 2100, and every increase in our knowledge of her- edity made the eugenic advantages of artificial insemination more obvious. Moreover, the growth of education and the rise in native intelligence due to pioneer eugenic programs steadily reduced opposition to all eugenic measures."

"You indicated that eugenic progress had been largely but not entirely voluntary. What compulsory methods were used?" I asked.

"During the 21st century a growing number of countries adopted the policy of compulsory steriliza- tion of all seriously defective children before they became sexually mature. Moreover, compulsory steril- ization of all major or chronic criminals, all insane persons, all alcoholics and drug addicts, and some other smaller classes of seriously handicapped

-23-

persons was gradually adopted throughout the world. Such compulsory sterilization never affected more than 10% of the adult population, and many of those sterilized had already had one or more children, but it sharply reduced the number of normal children raised by unfit or unemployable parents, as well as reducing the number of eugenically inferior children."

"In my day," I remarked, "there was some talk of eugenics, but critics argued vigorously that no one was capable of deciding what our eugenic goals should be and that no government had the right to compel people to adopt eugenic marriage and child-bearing policies. How did you answer or convert such critics?"

"Both objections were scientifically invalid, but, for political reasons, we initially adopted eugenic policies which were not subject to these objections. We provided a wide variety of sperm cells and allowed each couple to choose the kind of offspring they desired. We found, as we expected, that in time nearly all parents-to-be voluntarily chose to have children who would be superior to themselves in appearance, health, and native intelligence. And, since the program was voluntary, no one could complain of state coercion on eugenic goals or methods."

"Do you use intelligence tests in your eugenic programs?" I asked. "They were subject to much criticism in my time."

"Some of that criticism was justified," Bee Four noted. "But, of course, intelligence tests have been greatly improved since 1980. We require all sperm donors to have high I.Q.s, as well as superior health and appearance. Moreover, we have developed new tests for creativity and emotional maturity on which we place equal reliance."

"How would your population rank if tested by our primitive intelligence tests?" I asked.

"We have actually given such tests in order to obtain data on very long run trends," Bee Four explained. "As a result, we know that our population has an average I.Q. of over 200 by your old Stanford-Binet test."

"You have achieved such high levels of physical and mental heredity that continued eugenic progress would seem to be little needed," I observed. "Do many people still use artificial insemination for eugenic reasons?"

"Indeed they do," Bee Four answered. "Since

your time we have discovered many thousands of harmful genes, which take a long time to eliminate.
Moreover, background radiation, partly a result of your nuclear weapons, damages many human genes every year. Thus, some eugenic measures are always needed merely to prevent deterioration of the human gene pool. And we still want to improve it each year. We believe there is no physical limit to further eugenic progress. Consequently, voluntary artificial insemination is more widely practiced today than ever before. But of course the rate of eugenic progress is much slower."

7. A Sightseeing Aircraft

At this point I was surprised to notice a dark shadow spreading rapidly over the roof garden beside me and then over the ground near the hospital. The sky had been cloudless the last time I had observed it. When I looked aloft to see what had obscured the sun, I was startled by the sight of an immense dirigible moving slowly and silently across the sky only a few hundred feet above me. It appeared to be over a thousand feet long and over two hundred feet wide.
"What on earth is that?" I asked.
"It is one of our sightseeing aircraft," Bee Four said. "Southern California still attracts an enormous number of tourists, and they can see and learn far more from a sightseeing tour in a low-flying slow-moving dirigible than from buses traveling along city streets. It can fly over nearby hills, bays, and beaches as well as over urban districts, and passengers can stretch their legs and vary their views of the city by walking around the spacious decks."
"But," I objected, "isn't there a serious risk that the airship will fall or be blown down on a populated urban area and cause a large number of casualties?"
"There is some slight danger in all forms of transport, but the airship is now safer than the airplane. The gas bag is divided into a dozen compartments, so that a hole in one or two would merely cause it to descend slowly and safely. The gas, of course, is non-combustible, and the motors and controls are much more powerful and reliable than those you had. Moreover, there are many open areas in the greenbelts which run through and around every city, so that an airship has many possible emergency landing sites throughout the city. Finally, sightseeing

dirigibles do not go aloft when the weather is windy,
rainy, or otherwise unsuitable."

"Do you use dirigibles for long-distance passenger travel?"

"Only for those travelers who wish to view the
countryside more clearly and carefully, and only
when the weather is favorable. Over 90% of long-
distance passengers travel by airplane or train."

At this point Bee Four suggested that we return
to my hospital room to avoid overtaxing my still
limited strength, and I consented because, though
still fascinated by the incredible cityscape around
me, I did feel quite tired.

After I had again settled myself in my comfortable bed, and had had another meal and medical examination, I resumed my questioning of Bee Four.

8. About Bee Four

"You have been caring for me most considerately
for several days now," I said to Bee Four, "and you
have told me much about the strange new world around
me, but you have told me almost nothing about yourself. Why were you chosen to introduce me to this
world?"

"I was assigned to you because I am the senior
local specialist in the language and culture of the
region and time in which you lived. The language you
speak is a dead language today, one which few historians speak."

"Why did you decide to specialize in my age and
language?"

"I became a historian because my parents were
historians and because I had always enjoyed reading
history. I chose to specialize in the language and
culture of Southern California because I was born
here. And my graduate advisor persuaded me to specialize in your era because he thought it had been
neglected."

"What universities did you attend?" I enquired.

"I did all of my undergraduate and graduate work
at the University of California, which ranks as high
today as in your time. I obtained a doctoral degree
in what we call Early American History in the year
356, new era. I wrote a thesis on the major American
social trends of your century."

"Did you say 356?" I asked, surprised.

"Yes, 356, post world union."

"But then you must be 84 years old," I remarked,
and you look little over 40. Are you unusual in this

respect?"

"No, I do not think so. I merely illustrate the great benefits of eugenic progress since your time."

"Do you have a husband and children?"

"Yes, I have a husband, a fellow historian, whom I met when a student, and I have two daughters, both of whom are historians. My husband is doing some field research in a region you called Pakistan, but he will be home in a month or two."

"Is it not very unusual for four members of a family to have the same profession?" I asked.

"It is unusual, but far more common than in your era. We have learned that children who take up the profession of a parent are more likely to excel in their field because they learn much from their parent, or, better yet, parents, as well as from their professors and books. Moreover, husband and wife teams can carry out research projects which no single person could, and they have common interests which make married life more satisfying and enduring."

9. Names

"You have never told me your full name," I said to Bee Four. "What is your last name, and do you have a middle name?"

"We have numbers and symbols which, in combination, serve as names also," she replied. "My first name is not spelt "Before" or "Bee Four," as you have probably assumed. It is spelt capital letter B, plus Arabic number 4, and these two symbols are only the first two of the six symbols in my full name or number. My full name or number is B4-$\overline{AB}$-91. We use 10 Arabic numerals, and all letters of the alphabet in our names, and each symbol may or may not be underlined or overlined, so that there are over 150 possible symbols for use in each symbol space. As a result, we can name and distinguish over 10 trillion different persons without using more than six symbols in any name. Our name-numbers replace all the different identification numbers you used on credit cards, automobile license plates, social security records, passports, and so forth. Since only one person in some 20,000 has a name-number beginning with the same two symbols, we use the first two symbols for all informal social intercourse. The full name-number is used only on legal documents, tax returns, and other items where precise identification is necessary. It is also tattooed on the right

thigh and right arm of every child before he is one
year old so that his precise identity will always be
easily determinable."

"But doesn't the use of such name-numbers dehu-
manize people?" I asked. "In my day we already anti-
cipated and feared the replacement of names by
numbers."

"Yes, I have read of your fears in our history
books," B4 (to use her true name) replied. "But
human feelings arise from contacts between people,
not from contacts between names. When names stimulate emotions, it is because they are associated with
certain people. And, when numbers become associated
with people, they arouse similar emotions. We can
depersonalize the world only by changing people and
their behavior, not by changing names or identification numbers.

"Moreover, in your day you were already using
billions of identification numbers because they are
necessary for efficient administration. We have
merely simplified your complex and conflicting system
of personal identification, and have thereby saved
many billions of hours of labor."

"But if you use identification numbers for
names," I resumed, "how can the public identify members of the same family?"

"They can't," she said, "but there are compen-
sating advantages. Women do not have to change
their name when they marry or remarry, and children
do not have to decide whether to take their mother's
or their father's surname. Moreover, even your name
system did not identify any ancestors or relatives on
the mother's side of the family. As some of your
contemporaries had already begun to proclaim, your
naming system was sexist or male chauvinist."

"Don't you even distinguish males from females?"
I asked.

"We do distinguish them," she answered. "The
first symbol of all male numbers is underlined. The
first symbol of female numbers is not."

10. My First Voca Lesson

After a long pause, B4 changed the subject of
conversation.

"I think it is time for you to begin to learn
our language which we call Voca. It is a new language scientifically designed to make it easily teach-
able and learnable. Every sound is represented by a
separate letter of our enlarged and redesigned

alphabet. Partly for this reason, and partly because of eugenic reform, our children begin to learn
reading at age 2, and can read at your eighth-grade
level by age 5. We have no textbooks designed for
survivors from your century, so we will start you off
with the first reader we give our two-year olds.
Nearly all the words are illustrated by pictures, so
you will need no dictionary to begin your study."

    With that, she rose from her chair, picked up a
book on a nearby table, and brought it over to me.

    When I opened it and began to leaf through it,
I discovered that it looked very much like a first-
grade reader of my time. I spent the next hour
studying this colorful text, and after supper I resumed my study, but soon became sleepy and put it
aside. I fell asleep almost imediately.

CHAPTER III

MY THIRD DAY ON THE HOSPITAL ROOF

When I awoke the next day, it again took me several minutes to orient myself. It was the sight of
the calendar on the wall and its unbelievable year
number, 411, which helped most to remind me of where
I was and what had happened. As my memory came back,
a feeling of euphoria again swept over me. What a
fortunate man I was! What a vast number of questions
I still had to ask! How eager I was to view again
the startling garden city which surrounded me! And
how hungry I was! At this thought I promptly rang
the nurse's bell to hasten the delivery of my breakfast. My charming nurse, DD, soon appeared in person, a little later my breakfast, and then B4 and
the handsome doctors for my daily medical exam, which
I apparently passed.
       Soon afterwards, B4 again guided me to the ele-
vator which took us to the hospital roof garden,
where we settled down near the outside wall, so that
I could have a good view of the city around us. The
day was sunny and smogless. The whole city looked
like a garden with a few buildings scattered among
the tall trees. I again noted with pleasure that
every building whose roof I could see was crowned by
a roof garden full of plants, garden furniture, and
colorful umbrellas.
       As I studied the magnificent garden city around
me, I re-reviewed in my mind all that B4 had told me
about city planning. Then my mind shifted to another
subject. For the first time I became curious about
the world outside this model city.

1.   The North American Government

       "Is California still one of fifty states in an
independent United States of America?" I asked.
       "No, all state governments have been eliminated.
They were established in a day when it took the
average citizen far longer to reach his state capital
than it now takes him to reach the world capital in
Hawaii. State governments were already obsolete in
your day, but it took another hundred years to get
rid of them. Today national capitals play the political and administrative role in the world federal
union that state capitals played in the American

-30

federal union in your time. They are a concession to regional prejudices and loyalties and a means of decentralizing administration."

"But in my century," I said, "many independent countries were much smaller and/or less populous than the state of California. Are they still on the same administrative level as the U.S.?"

"Of course not. All small and intermediate-size nations have been merged into 12 large super states. North America, from Panama north, is now a single nation. So are South America, Europe, North Africa, Sub-Saharan Africa, North India, South India, North China, South China, Japan-Korea, South Asia, Western Asia, and Australasia. Each of these nations has a population of over 100 million and less than 300 million."

"What is the population of the U.S. now?" I asked.

"The part of North America you knew as the U.S. now has about 240 million inhabitants, and over one third of them live in the territory you called California. The new state of North America has a population of almost 300 million."

"Apparently the population of Asia has fallen very greatly" I remarked.

"Yes, it is now less than half the size it was in your day," B4 said.

"You say that American state governments have been abolished. In my time most progressive political scientists advocated transfer of many local public functions to state governments. Why were they mistaken?" I asked.

"They had the right idea, centralization of government, but did not carry it far enough. We have completely abolished local government as well as state or provincial government in all countries. We do not believe that traffic laws, criminal laws, civil laws, educational methods, spending per pupil, and health care should differ from city to city or state to state. And we have learned that large-scale professional management is more efficient than small-scale lay management of public agencies. Therefore, all North American schools are now managed by a single national Department of Education, all health care agencies are now managed by a single national Department of Health, and so forth."

"You astonish me," I said. "We thought that local self government was an absolutely essential feature of a free and democratic society. It placed government close to the people. We believed that local voters were more interested in, and more qualified to solve, local problems than legislators or bureaucrats in distant state and national offices."

"But you just explained that your progressive political scientists were already advocating much centralization," B4 countered. "And in fact by 1980 many functions once performed by your local governments had already been shifted to state and national agencies. This well-established trend continued in all countries throughout the 21st and 22nd centuries. Local self-government was inefficient and harmful not only because it was often small-scale and always resulted in unjustified local differences in laws and public services, but also because it permitted and encouraged local voters and officials to place local interests above national interests. For instance, nearly all your local governments discriminated against workers and businessmen who lived outside their area. They prepared elaborate and uneconomic building codes designed to favor local contractors, workers, and building materials. Their tax laws and tax enforcement policies discriminated against nonresident property owners. In fact, most local laws and policies were discriminatory. And one of the principal activities of all local governments was the continuous effort to secure larger financial grants from state and federal agencies, at the expense of competing claimants."

"But surely local voters were more interested in and familiar with their own local problems than were state and national legislators," I protested.

"That was one of the most widely accepted political myths of your time," B4 countered. "The data on voting turnouts shows that many more of your voters voted in national than in local elections. And your press and broadcasters gave voters much fuller and more accurate information about national issues than about local issues. That is one reason your local police and politicians were much more corrupt than your national police and politicians. Today, all local police and other local administrators are constantly supervised by regional executives of their own profession, and regional executives by national ones. Thus every local official is supervised by a fellow professional fully competent to oversee his work. Your elected local mayors were rarely competent to supervise professional services, and were themselves unsupervised."

"It seems to me," I remarked, "that nearly all of your objections to local and provincial self-

government also apply to national self-government.
For instance, should not laws on crime, marrige, inheritance, education, etc., be uniform in all nations,
as well as in all regions within a nation?"

"Yes, they should and sometime they will be, but
nations still differ widely in average real wages,
average education, average health, etc., and the most
advanced nations are still unwilling to subsidize
less advanced nations enough to make the same laws
and social policies feasible and suitable in all
nations."

2. The Evolution of World Government

"Is the U.S. still an independent nation, or is
it merely a province of a world state?" I asked.

"It is a largely self-governing province of a
world state, the World Federal Union (WFU). The
position of the U.S. in the WFU corresponds closely
to the position of the state of California in the
U.S. of your day."

"Does that mean that the U.S. is unable to restrict immigration, foreign investment, and foreign
trade?"

"It can still control immigration, but not foreign investment and trade. When the WFU was formed,
the advanced nations were unwilling to surrender control over immigration for fear of having their wage
levels and living standards depressed by mass immigration from poorer countries. But the WFU has full
control over foreign trade and investment, and has
enforced free trade throughout the world."

"Are there still wide differences in real wages
between different countries?" I asked.

"Yes, but even the poorest countries enjoy living standards well above those of the U.S. in 1980."

"In my day," I resumed, "the U.S., the U.S.S.R.,
and many other nations were steadily expanding their
military forces and/or armaments. At least five
nations already possessed nuclear weapons. Moreover,
the cold war had continued so long that few if any
American or Russian leaders were able to deal
rationally with the problems which divided the two
superpowers. In both countries those dissenters who
advocated appeasement were likely to be blacklisted,
ostracized, and/or imprisoned. I am especially eager
to learn how you ended the cold war and created a
strong world government. Was it achieved by peaceful
agreement among most or all nations, or was it
achieved by military force?"

"It took a little of both," B4 answered. "During the first half of the 21st century the two superpowers established a condominium which used threats of military force and trade embargoes to compel all other nations to surrender their nuclear arms and to convert or destroy their nuclear-arms plants."

"Just how did this happen," I asked.

"The principal cause of the creation of the condominium was the continuing rise in the number of minor nuclear powers. In the last decade of your century some of the Moslem states finally secured a few nuclear bombs and threatened to use them against Israel. This almost caused the outbreak of a third world war, but the U.S and the U.S.S.R. finally agreed on a joint occupation and disarmament of Israel and the Arab countries involved. Later, when a revolutionary nationalistic government assumed power in Pakistan and began to prepare for a nuclear attack on India, the two superpowers found it necessary to occupy and disarm Pakistan. Both of these cooperative occupations of foreign territory created very difficult problems of joint administration and control. To end such problems and to assure nuclear disarmament of all other nations except the U.S. and U.S.S.R., the governments of the two superpowers divided the entire world into two zones of control, the American and the Soviet, and each power authorized the other to enforce nuclear disarmament and peace in its zone, with the assistance of the other superpower when needed and requested. The American zone included Canada, Latin America, Australasia, Africa, and Western Europe. The Soviet zone included Eastern Europe and Asia."

"We believed that the creation of such a condominium would be a gross violation of the right of each nation to be completely free and independent," I objected.

"It is of course true," B4 replied, "that both the rise of the Russo-American Condominium and the subsequent creation of a democratic world government restricted the freedom and independence of most or all states, but such a restriction was essential to the prevention of nuclear war. In all such cases, the end justifies the means."

"But surely the creation of such zones of control greatly increased the military power of each of the superpowers and made the danger and possible costs of war between them far greater than before," I argued.

"Yes, it did increase the potential losses from

-34-

a Russo-American War," B4 conceded, "but it made such
a war much less likely by ruling out a collision between Soviet and American military forces in any
country. The Condominium Agreement determined in
advance whose forces should intervene in each country. Moreover, it gave each superpower so large an
area to control and develop that both were fully
occupied for many decades. During these decades both
major countries gradually became more alike and more
tolerant of the other. The U.S.S.R. became much more
prosperous and democratic. The U.S. became much more
socialist and much less fearful of communism. As a
result, by the end of the 21st century, they were
working together in the World Federal Union, the
successor to the United Nations."

"Do you mean that the world government is still
controlled by the U.S. and the U.S.S.R.?" I asked.

"No. They did control it for over a century,
but the resulting long duration of peace and economic
growth reduced international tension so much that the
superpowers felt safe in allowing the world government to become more and more democratic. And belief
in, and the practice of, government by experts grew
steadily during these years, both within each of the
superpowers and in the World Federal Union."

"In my day," I remarked, "we thought we had
learned that it was very difficult for a superpower
to dominate even a single small backward state like
Korea, Vietnam, or Afganistan. How then did it become possible for the condominium to dominate the
entire third world?"

"It was difficult for the United States to control and pacify Korea and Viet Nam only because the
U.S.S.R. and China actively supported native armies
fighting against the U.S. Indeed, the chief purpose
of U.S. intervention was to prevent Soviet domination
of these countries. As soon as the U.S. and the
U.S.S.R. began to work together, all hope of success-
ful resistance to them ended."

"But surely China and India, each with a population larger than that of the U.S. and the U.S.S.R.
combined, were serious threats to world domination
by these superpowers,." I countered. "How did the
condominium control them?"

"During the era when the condominium became dominant, China and India were so handicapped by over-
population and recurring famine that they could not
offer serious resistance. And the condominium
threatened these countries with destruction of some
of their major cities if they did not surrender their

nuclear weapons and permit continuous inspection of
their munitions plants and military installations.
Moreover, the condominium guaranteed both nations
against attack. Hence, they yielded to the condominium demands, but only after a brief blockade by
land, air, and water, and the annihilation of one
Chinese city."

"How does the world government prevent the
secret production of nuclear arms and other aggressive weapons in individual states whose rulers might
want to rule the world?" I asked.

"The World Federal Union has a special secret
service whose sole function is to detect the illegal
production, storage, and use in military training of
prohibited weapons. It uses highly sensitive detect-
ors mounted on surveillance satellites, commercial
planes,and land vehicles. It also has secret agents
in all states, and offers large rewards for information concerning the manufacture of illegal weapons.
These measures are now needed more to prevent the use
of such weapons by individual groups of criminals and
fanatics than to prevent national or social revolu-
tions. In the 21st century there were several cases
in which terrorists tried to obtain nuclear bombs and
use them to hold entire cities up for ransom. These
efforts helped to build popular support for Soviet-
American cooperation in controlling nuclear weapons."

3. Government by Experts

"Is the world government now democratic?" I
asked.

"No, it is not. In the first century of its
existence it was undemocratic because the two superpowers insisted that they should be able to dominate
it. In the next century it remained undemocratic
chiefly because the citizens of advanced countries
were unwilling to be ruled by a world government
dominated by backward countries. But the participation of other states in world government grew steadily during these centuries. The world government,
like the North American government, is undemocratic
today because nearly all people now believe that
government by experts, i.e., by social scientists,
is far more efficient than democratic government.
The members of all legislatures—world and national—
are now chosen directly or indirectly, by professional associations of social scientists. And the
legislatures choose all chief executives from the
ranks of eminent, professionally-trained public

administrators. Today, we have as much confidence in
social scientists and social engineers as you in your
day had in doctors of medicine. We consider it as
unreasonable for untrained men to vote on methods of
economic stabilization or taxation as for them to
vote on methods of treating cancer or heart disease.
Of course, the enormous growth of knowledge in the
field of social science since your time is a major
reason for this change in attitude. In your day,
social scientists were almost as ignorant and incompetent as doctors and surgeons had been in 1800.
They were not even able to advise governments well on
how to prevent or cure the Great Depression of 1930
to 1940. Only World War II finally forced the American government to temporarily spend enough to create
near-full employment. And, after World War II, your
economists were unable to tell governments how to
avoid price inflation without causing serious unemployment."

"In our day," I countered, "we feared that any
ruling class or elite would use political agencies
and laws to exploit the people for their own private
benefit. How did you avoid this evil?"

"We have prevented such exploitation chiefly by
limiting the incomes of all government officials. No
official is paid a salary more than twice as high as
that of the average worker, and none can have any
other income. Moreover, all personal income passes
through national banks. Thus there is little opportunity for, and little benefit from, political corruption or exploitation."

"But," I persisted, "how do you prevent your
rulers from becoming dictators and arbitrarily ending
such limitations on their power and wealth?"

"We use precisely the same methods democratic
countries used in your day. In our schools we teach
all young people how harmful it would be to overthrow
or subvert our form of government. Moreover, we
practice a separation of powers. We not only have
independent courts and independent media of information, but also have military and police forces, whose
heads are appointed and removed by legislatures, not
by chief executives. And, the top executives of all
key agencies serve for limited terms and cannot be
reappointed. Finally, the kind of men chosen for
high political office by professional social scientists are not the kind of men who wish to become
dictators and abandon scientific principles of government."

4. Overpopulation

"In my time," I remarked, "many people feared that the rapid growth in world population would soon cause widespread famine. And some even predicted that famine in backward countries would drastically reduce their raw material exports and stop economic progress in advanced countries. Did their predictions come true?" I asked.

"No, they did not," B4 replied. "Of course there was chronic starvation and malnutrition among the poorest classes in most undeveloped countries throughout the 20th and 21st centuries, as there had been throughout all previous centuries, and there were occasional regional famines in Asia and Africa, but such misfortunes never significantly reduced the population of any country or seriously curtailed the imports of raw materials by advanced states. On the other hand, the continued growth of population throughout the 21st century did restrict the rate of economic progress in every country, and this brake on economic progress prolonged the misery and poverty of billions of people, chiefly in backward countries."

"How did you finally stop the rapid growth of world population?" I asked.

"Largely by applying more generally and effectively the knowledge already available in your day," she replied. "There were many later improvements in technique, but your contemporaries already knew enough about various methods of birth control—contraception, sterilization, and abortion—to limit the population to any desired degree. And birth rates in advanced countries had long been falling. During the 21st century, birth rates in backward countries fell even faster than those in advanced countries had fallen during the 20th century. Of course, this rapid decline was too late and too slow, but it did finally permit backward countries to more than double their economic growth rates."

"Have the peoples of once backward countries been able to achieve the standard of living found in advanced countries?" I asked.

"Indeed they have not," she answered. "Economic progress has continued in all advanced countries, so that the absolute margin of difference between living standards, is still very wide, but this difference is far less significant and divisive. All countries have achieved average real incomes as high as Americans of your day enjoyed, and they spend their personal and government incomes much more wisely.

"Unfortunately, the reckless and wasteful depletion of irreplaceable natural resources—especially
petroleum, natural gas and nonferrous metals—due to
rapid industrialization and population growth during
the 20th century made it very difficult for backward
nations to industrialize during the 21st century.
They eventually found it necessary not only to end
their population growth but to radically reduce their
total population. Moreover, later, most advanced
countries also adopted a policy of gradual population
reduction in order to maintain their high rates of
progress in real income per person."

"What is the total world population today?" I
asked.

"About three billion," she replied. "During the
21st century it reached a peak of over 8 billion, but
it has declined steadily ever since, most rapidly in
Asia, where the population is now less than one third
that of your day. The current World Federal Union
population plan calls for a continuing gradual reduction in population, chiefly in Asia."

"How do you control the birth rate," I asked.

"We rely primarily on education and propaganda,
but some 10% of all American women are required to be
sterilized for eugenic reasons before they have any
children. The majority of women have only two children and then request sterilizatin for themselves and/
or their husbands. Sterilization of mothers is compulsory after the birth of a third child, unless they
have been exempted for eugenic reasons."

5. Food Supplies

At this point I arose and walked slowly around
the perimeter of the roof garden again, marveling all
the while at the incredible panorama and wondering
whether I was dreaming or awake. When I reached my
wheel-chair again, B4 noted that it was time for
lunch, and asked if I would care to dine at the gaily
decorated outdoor cafe in the center of the roof garden. Being tired of hospital beds and meals, I
readily assented, and we seated ourselves at a garden
table. The menu was not only in a strange foreign
language but the language used a strange alphabet. I
had to rely on B4's translation, but I was soon eating a vegetable stew with dark lumps in it that
tasted a little like beef. B4, after a moment's hes-
itation, had translated the name of my main course as
"synthetic beef stew."

"What is a synthetic beef stew?" I asked.

"It's a protein-rich meat substitute," she replied. "We eat almost no real meat. Even in your day, meat cost more than twice as much per gram of protein as any vegetable food, and the cost difference is much greater today. We have learned how to make synthetic protein out of wood, corn stocks, and other cheap raw material. We have a greater variety of protein-rich foods than you had, and they cost less than one quarter as much per gram of protein as meat costs today."

"But didn't Americans complain bitterly when you deprived them of ham sandwiches, pork sausages, hamburgers, and other popular meat products?" I asked.

"The process was so gradual it was hardly noticed," B4 replied. "The cost of meat products rose faster than the cost of meat substitutes for centuries, and the quality of meat substitutes improved steadily. We have never had to use any coercion or rationing to reduce the consumption of meat or any other harmless product. We still rely almost entirely on price changes. Of course, educational advertising has also helped."

6. Free Distribution

"In my century," I remarked, "many socialists preached that food and other necessities of life should eventually become free goods, i.e., should be provided free of charge in order to assure a good life for all. How were they wrong?"

"They failed to realize that most free goods are consumed carelessly and wastefully, especially food. Moreover, there are many kinds of food, and if all were free, most people would order only the most costly. It would, of course, be impossible to meet the demand for gourmet foods if they were free."

"But wouldn't it be desirable to make the least expensive foods, like bread and potatoes, free goods in order to guarantee a minimum supply of food to all?"

"No, because this would promote waste of such foods, as well as undue consumption of them. We assure an adequate diet for all adults by giving all of them an adequate money income. This permits them to choose rationally among alternative foods by comparing the prices they pay with the want satisfaction they receive. Such rational calculation is impossible when goods are free."

"But," I objected, "your last argument seems to

rule out free provision of education and health care, which were already largely free in my time."

"Education and health care are personal services rendered by professionals who are the best judges of what services we need, and who can personally prevent waste of the free services they provide. Food is a tangible good which is much more easily wasted. Moreover, consumers are the best judges of which foods please them, but not of which drugs cure them. For these and other reasons, the case for free distribution of basic education and health care is sound, while the case for free distribution of food is unsound."

"Are education and health care the only free goods now?" I enquired.

"No indeed," B4 answered. "Almost half of all consumers' goods are provided free of charge. All radio and television broadcasts, all child care, all legal services, all police and fire protection, all insurance, etc., are free goods. Moreover, education and health care alone account for over 20% of U.S. GNP."

7. Racial Homogenization

After lunch, B4 and I circled the roof once slowly, and settled on the west side. Soon I resumed my questioning.

"I have noticed no negroes in this hospital," I remarked. "In my era Los Angeles had a large negro population, and many hospital employees were negroes. What has become of them?"

"They have been entirely absorbed in the general population by intermarriage with whites," B4 explained. "Even in your era the average California negro was over one quarter Caucasian by ancestry. Now the average American white is about 4% negro by race. That is a major reason why nearly all of them now have what looks like a suntan. You probably thought it was the product of the California sun, but in fact it is largely the result of the racial assimilation of your black and brown-skinned minorities."

"How long did this process of racial homogenization take?" I asked.

"It is still going on, but is 90% complete in California."

"How did you reduce or end white prejudice against miscegenation?" I asked. "In my time this prejudice was still very strong."

"It was based upon the memory of slavery, which

gradually faded away, and upon great differences in
the color, education, and average income of the two
races. These differences diminished slowly as miscegenation and social reform became more and more
effective. By 2200 A.D. the average levels of education and income among American negroes were almost as
high as those of whites. Moreover, most negroes were
then light brown rather than black in skin color. As
a result, white prejudice against intermarriage with
negroes virtually disappeared, and intermarriage
became very common."

"You said that racial integration is the chief
reason nearly all of the local population has a tan
skin. What are the other major reasons?"

"Continuing immigration from Mexico and other
Latin American nations has been another important
cause. And local eugenic factors have also played a
significant role."

"How could local eugenic factors affect complexion preference and racial intermarriage?" I asked,
incredulously.

"The sunny climate of California is not suited
to either extreme blondes or extreme blacks. That is
why evolution developed blonde races only in the
extreme North and blacks only in the tropics. It was
human migration that brought both Nordic blondes and
African blacks to the more temperate and desirable
climatic areas like California. Moreover, blacks
suffered from racial prejudice in all regions where
they were a minority. Therefore, when the development and popularization of voluntary artificial
insemination made it possible for parents to choose
the complexion, as well as the degree of health and
intelligence, of their offspring, more and more blonde
and black parents chose to have children slightly
less blonde or black than themselves. Over the past
400 years this voluntary eugenic evolution has helped
to produce a more homogeneous race in every climatic
zone. Here the new race is a light brown because
that shade of skin is best suited to the climate.
However in Northern Europe, Canada, and Siberia,
blue-eyed blondes are as common as they ever were in
those areas, and in most tropical areas the native
population is as black or brown as ever."

"Your explanation seems to me to imply that the
great majority of Americans now live and work in the
cities or regions they were born in," I countered.
"In my era there were vast domestic migrations within, as well as large-scale immigration into, the
U.S."

-42-

"Your inference is correct. There is now little internal migration. We have learned that most people are happier and more productive living among old friends and relatives in their place of birth than when living and working elsewhere. Migration and immigration were important causes of crime and mental disease in your era. Almost every American town or city is now planned and managed so as to provide suitable jobs for nearly all residents. As a result, our population is relatively immobile."

8.   Immigration

"In my time," I said, "many millions of poor, dark, or brown-skinned people were eager to emigrate from their backward mother countries to the much more advanced countries of North-West Europe and North America. And the population of poor countries was not only four or five times as large as the population of the countries to which they wished to immigrate, but was also growing two or three times as fast. How was this serious threat to the economic welfare of advanced peoples solved?"

"I have mentioned the rapid adoption of effective birth control in backward countries during the 21st century," B4 replied. "However, that did not end the threat of heavy immigration into advanced countries. Shortly after you began your long hibernation, one advanced country after another was forced to restrict radically all immigration from poor countries. Great Britain, France, and Germany prohibited nearly all such immigration before 2000 A.D., and the U.S. followed their example soon afterwards. Illegal immigration was ended by requiring all job-seekers to show proof of legal residence. Ever since then, all advanced countries have limited total net immigration from poorer countries to less than 0.1% of domestic population per year. If they had not radically limited such immigration, their real-wage growth rates would have been radically reduced, or would even have become negative."

"But wouldn't it be socially desirable to make real incomes more equal throughout the world by permitting and encouraging more immigration from poorer to richer countries?" I objected. "In my time nearly all progressive thinkers believed that income differences should be reduced both within and between nations."

"On this point I agree with you," she said. "But it is still politically impossible to persuade

-43-

the voters in rich nations to give up their personal
economic advantages in order to radically reduce
income differences among nations. They still fear
that poorer peoples would start to breed recklssly
again. And they feel that they deserve the rewards
produced by their ancestors' thrift and birth control."

"I thought you had government by experts, not by
voters,"

"Yes, but the experts are careful to heed the
wishes of their people on such basic, emotional
issues."

At this point B4 paused and began to examine me
rather carefully. "I fear you have become tired,"
she said. "I think we should cease talking and
return to your room."

"Yes, I think I am tired," I said, "though this
new world is so exciting that I hate to leave it even
for a moment."

"We will have ample time to study it in the
future," she said, and began to wheel me towards the
elevator. When we reached my room, she insisted that
I rest without talking. I listened to soft music for
a while, but soon fell asleep. When I awoke, I
studied my elementary Voca reader until supper, and
again afterwards.

CHAPTER IV

ANOTHER DAY ON TOP

The next morning, after my breakfast and a medical examination, B4 again took me to the hospital roofgarden, where we settled down in a new place near the railing, with a perfect view of a different part of Los Angeles. It was another perfect smogless day. I marvelled anew at the quiet colorful garden city around us. I could not hear the sound of a single vehicle or construction project. I felt as if I would never tire of gazing at the incredible panorama around me. B4 must have understood my feelings, for she allowed me to observe and meditate in silence for some time. She had brought a book to read. Every once in a while I suggested a move to a different viewpoint, so that I could study a different part of the city. I also left my wheelchair occasionally to stretch and strengthen my legs, which were becoming stronger each day.

1. Voca and English

After a while I sat down beside B4 and asked, "What kind of a book are you reading?"

"It is a history of North America since your time," she said. "I am trying to prepare myself for some of the questions you may ask me."

"As a result of my first elementary lessons in your new world language I am curious as to its nature and history," I remarked. "What is the origin of this language, and why and when did you adopt it?"

"Our language is called Voca. As the name suggests, it was largely designed and named by persons speaking languages with many Latin roots, but it is in fact an almost entirely new language, one carefully designed by language scientists so as to enable people to speak, write, and think far more rapidly and clearly than ever before."

"But how can any new language enable people to think faster and better?" I asked.

"When we think, we think in words. We talk to ourselves, and such talk involves incipient muscular movements in the throat and mouth, as when we read silently. The shorter the words and sentences, the less the muscular movement, and the faster the process of thought becomes. Moreover, every grammatical and vocabulary reform that enables us to speak or write more clearly also enables us to think more clearly."

"In my day," I observed, "some futurists predicted that English would soon become the world language. They noted that far more scientific and technical literature was being published in English than in any other language, that the British Empire had spread the use of English through wide areas of Africa and Asia; that American military forces were spread around the globe, that English and American firms dominated world trade; that English and American movies and TV programs were being shown around the world, and that English-speaking tourists far outnumbered those from any other language area. Why didn't English become the new world language?"

"As a matter of fact it did," B4 said. "By the year 2050, almost every college graduate in non-English speaking countries had to be able to read English in order to keep up with the new literature in his field, most of which was published only in English. Translation of most scientific books and journal articles into minor languages had already become uneconomic, and translation into major languages was costly and slow. By 2100 A.D. nearly all university courses in advanced science, technology, medicine, and history in non-English-speaking countries were taught in English, and English had become the only language used in international trade and communication.

"Incidentally, the rapid spread of English in the 21st century was greatly aided by reforms in its alphabet, which was increased from 26 to 45 letters to allow a separate letter for every sound, and by reforms in its spelling, which changed the spelling of every word to reflect its pronunciation in standard English. These reforms made it very much easier for children of English-speaking parents to learn to read and write English, as well as making it easier for all non-English-speaking adults to learn to read and write English."

"If English had already become a world language, why didn't you reform it further instead of inventing a new language?" I asked.

"The decision to adopt a new world language was made about 300 years ago," B4 explained. "The chief reasons were that most English words were considered too long and too obscurely related to each other, that English grammar was too complex, and that English conjugations were irregular. In Voca the 40 most common words consist of one letter only, some

600 of the most common words consist of two letters
only, and no non-compound words have more than five
or six letters. All conjugations are perfectly regular, and no word has more than one meaning. For
these and other reasons, it should not take you very
long to learn to speak, read, and write Voca. As
soon as you have learned to understand and read Voca
you will be able to increase your knowledge of our
world very rapidly by reading and by looking at TV
programs."

"I can hardly wait to learn it. Your language
fascinates me. But how on earth were you able to
persuade or compel all Americans, let alone all
citizens of other countries, to adopt a new scientific language?" I asked. "In my day, language minorities clung to their ancient languages as emotionally
as they clung to their ancient religions, and each
nation speaking a major language was eager to spread
the use of its tongue."

"Voca was introduced first as a universal second
language," B4 replied. "Since English had been a
foreign language to most of those who used it as a
second or international language, they did not object
to its gradual replacement by Voca. Indeed, they
rather welcomed the implied slight to the often chau-
vinistic English-speaking peoples.

"After Voca had been universally adopted as a
second language, its use was gradually increased by
limiting higher education in other langauges, re-
stricting book and film production in other languages,
and requiring all newspapers, periodicals, and books
to adopt a small number of new Voca words each month
of each year. The process of introduction was carefully planned to be so gradual that it would arouse
only minor objection. No single generation had to
bear all or most of the burden of language reform.
Indeed, the complete worldwide adoption of Voca as a
native language took over 150 years.

2. B4's History Book

After this discussion of Voca, I got out of my
wheelchair, and, accompanied by B4, again made a slow
circuit of the large hospital roof garden. I felt
stronger and calmer than the day before. But I was
still exhilarated and enthralled by the panorama
around me. Innumerable questions ran through my
mind. I had to remind myself that no one could learn
everything about a strange society all at once.

When I returned to my wheelchair, B4's book again caught my eye, and I asked, "What do your historians consider the most importrant events of my age to have been?" I asked.

"Our historians pay far less attention to historical _events_ than yours did. They concentrae most of their attention on major long-run social _trends_. Our history books are full of statistical charts and tables. But they do mention World Wars I and II, the Russian Revolution, the Chinese Revolution, and the Nazi holocaust. I must say I was horrified to read again of the cold-blooded torture and murder of 12,000,000 persons, half Jews, in German concentration camps. That is the greatest atrocity on record in any literate country."

"And what does your book list as the major social trends in my century," I asked.

"Scientific, technological, economic and educational progress are treated as the most important, but the rise of socialism was also very important. You called the 18th century the age of reason. We call your century the age of science and technology, because progress in science and technology was more rapid in your age than ever before or since."

"And what does your book describe as the other major social trends of the 21st century," I enquired.

"All the major trends of the 20th century continued during the 21st, but they created far greater changes in Asia and Africa than in Europe and North America. The great changes which had occurred in Europe and North America during the 20th century took place in Asia and Africa during the 21st century, in which Asia and Africa were industrialized and westernized. By 2100 A.D., Asia was as literate and prosperous as Western Europe had been in 1900 A.D."

After this discussion, conversation lagged while I tried to review and organize in my mind the many facts I had been told. Before I had a chance to resume my questioning, B4 noted that it was time for lunch and led the way to a table under a colorful awning in the roof-garden cafe. While she studied the menu, a handsome man I recognized as my chief physician approached our table and greeted us. B4 introduced him to me as Dr. NT, and asked him to join us. After we had all ordered our lunch, he addressed himself to me. B4 translated.

"What do you think of our new Los Angeles?" he asked.

"It seems unbelievably clean, quiet, and beautiful," I replied. "You seem to have solved all of our problems without using any machines and techniques which were not already known in my time."

"That is largely true," Dr. NT remarked. "The chief obstacles to efficient urban and social organization in your day were ideological prejudices, not technological backwardness. But of course there has been great technological progress since your day."

3. Medical Care

"If I may change the subject," I ventured, "I would like to ask you how you cure cancer today."

"We have confirmed the suggestion advanced already in the 20th century that most cancers are caused by viruses. We have identified and cultured many cancer viruses and have learned how to prepare and use vaccines which prevent nearly all forms of cancer. All our children are vaccinated against most forms of cancer at an early age. Some of these vaccines are effective, if used properly with other with other drugs, on patients who already have a cancer. You were vaccinated successfully several days before you became conscious, so you have nothing to fear."

At this moment our waitress returned with our orders, so conversation lagged for a while. As soon as we had finished our light lunch and ordered drinks, I began to question the doctor again.

"I am most interested in your system of medical care," I began. "Could you tell me what are the chief differences between medical care in Los Angeles today and in my time?"

"The chief differences are that medical care today is universal and free, like public elementary education in your day. We do not allow people to avoid or escape essential medical care. From birth, each individual is required to submit to periodic medical, psychiatric, and dental examinations, and to accept treatment for any infectious or disabling disease. As a result, we diagnose most sicknes in a very early stage, nearly always before the patient is aware of it, and this permits us to treat and cure nearly all illness without hospitalization."

"If medical care is compulsory and universal, and if all families have high incomes, why should medical care be free?" I asked.

"Because the incidence of illness varies widely and this justifies some form of insurance. Free provision of medical care insures the individual against extraordinary medical bills without requiring

the expensive determination, collection, and distribution of health insurance premiums. In other words,
it is much more economic to raise existing taxes to
finance free health care than to create and collect
special health-insurance premiums. Moreover, when
doctors engaged in private medical practice and received fees for each medical service, they often
prescribed unnecessary services in order to increase
their income and/or avoid malpractice suits."

"In my time," I remarked, "many futurists predicted that group medical care in clinics would
eventually replace individual medical practice. Has
their prediction come true."

"Yes indeed," Dr. NT replied. "That change was
virtually completed before the middle of the 21st
century."

"Are patients allowed to choose their physicians
and dentists?" I asked.

"Not on their first visit to a clinic. We do
not believe patients know enough about medical care
or personnel to choose doctors wisely. And we do not
want our more charming doctors to work harder than
our less charming doctors. However, any patient who
is willing to pay a transfer fee may request that his
case be transferred to a different, unspecified
doctor, and nearly all such requests are soon granted."

"How long did you have to study to secure your
M.D. degree?" I enquired.

"Not as long as was necessary in your time. We
normally enter college at age 17 today, and medical
education is briefer and far more specalized. Thus
the eye doctor is taught nothing about most other
organs of the body. Also, we study ten months a
year, not eight as in your day. As a result,
although I obtained my M.D. at age 22, I have had two
or three times as many courses in my specialty as the
average specialist had completed in your time. Moreover, all doctors are now required to spend about 10%
of their time throughout their career in continuous
further postgraduate study."

"What is your medical specialty," I asked.

"I am a specialist in low temperature therapy
and, incidentally, in reviving persons drowned in
cold water. We sharply reduce the body temperature
of many patients to prepare them for major operations on the heart and the brain. This procedure
significantly reduces all activities of the body and
permits the surgeon to work more carefully and
slowly. Low-temperature specialists must of course

learn how to restore normal temperatures in the safest way. For this reason, we have been called upon to try to revive persons deep-frozen long ago."

"What are the chief causes of death now?" I queried.

"The chief cause of death today is suicide by the dying aged. As a result of eugenic and health care programs, very few people, less than 5%, die before age 90. And the great majority of those who learn that they are dying commit suicide just before or soon after they become bedfast."

"We considered suicide an immoral and cowardly act," I protested. "Why did men change their opinion on this subject?"

"As men became less religious, they became more considerate of the welfare of their relatives, friends, and fellow tax payers. In your era, those who died slow, painful deaths imposed heavy burdens on their families and on public agencies. A very substantial proportion of all health-care services was devoted to dying patients, and the emotional strain on relatives and friends was heavy. Moreover, as religious faith weakened, men came to fear divine punishment for suicide less and less."

"Do you mean that public opinion actually condones suicide?" I enquired.

"It does much more than condone suicide by the dying, it approves and applauds it because suicide reduces taxes as well as human suffering."

"Will you commit suicide?" I challenged.

"Of course," he answered. "I have no fear of a painless death. I only fear the possibly terrible pain of a slow death. The general acceptance of suicide by the dying has freed all men of this once near-universal fear."

"But suppose you have an unexpected stroke and become permanently paralyzed before you can kill yourself," I suggested.

"Like most persons, I have instructed my doctor to end my life, to practice active euthanasia, immediately after such a stroke, even if there is a possibility of partial recovery. I do not want to endure the pain of life as a helpless invalid, nor do I want to impose a heavy and useless cost on my family and friends. I want to die with dignity."

4. Drug Addiction

"In my time," I remarked, "the use of narcotics, tobacco, and alcoholic drinks ruined the health of

millions of Americans, and our costly and futile efforts to minimize the illegal trade in drugs filled
our prisons with drug addicts and dealers. How did
you solve these problems?"

"We developed a variety of addiction-control
measures, some of which affected all forms of harmful
addiction and some, certain forms only. Our first
and most general measure was to require producers of
legal addictive products to gradually reduce the
amount of the addictive element in their products.
For instance, we required all tobacco manufacturers
to reduce the amount of nicotine in each product by
1% every four months for many years. The change each
time was so small that few consumers ever felt any
pains of withdrawal and therefore few increased the
number of cigarettes they smoked. By this method the
consumption of all legal addictive products was, in
the long run, radically reduced without any direct
control of individual behavior."

"You surprise me," I said. "We had discussed
many proposals for addiction control, but no one ever
suggested that one. Moreover, its effects must have
seemed too gradual for most doctors. What other,
more quickly effective, measures did you use?"

"Early in the 21st century, by your calendar,
the U.S. Government permitted many doctors to provide
free or cheap narcotics to all heroin and cocaine
addicts. This sharply and immediately reduced the
amount of crime and the volume of illegal trade in
drugs. It also provided the government with the
names and addresses of all such addicts, which greatly facilitated subsequent efforts to re-educate and/
or detoxify these addicts. Eventually, all drug
addicts were required to undergo re-education and/or
detoxification, often more than once. Some were
compelled to consume control drugs, which made nar-
cotic consumption unpleasant."

"It must have been much more difficult to reduce
the consumption of alcohol and eliminate alcoholism"
I said. "We had tried prohibition from 1920 to 1933,
and it had failed to work."

"Yes, it was more difficult because there was,
initially, much less public support for control of
the use of alcoholic drinks. The U.S. government
began by prohibiting all forms of advertising for
such products. It also gradually increased excise
taxes on their producers, and used the additional
revenues to carry on an ever-growing educational campaign against the consumption of alcohol and to subsidize more and more detoxification centers. Eventu-

ally, about your year 2100 I believe, the production
of all alcoholic beverages was again prohibited, and
this time prohibition was effective because methods
of crime prevention had become far more sophisticated
and efficient."

After giving this answer, Dr. NT announced that
he had to return to his office, and left us. B4 and
I also left our table and returned to the edge of the
roof, so that I could survey the cityscape around the
hospital again. B4 began to point out and name the
more prominent and visible buildings and parks.
Nearly all the more distant buildings were hidden by
trees. But each of the nine surrounding towns had
two or three buildings of more than four stories, and
she explained their locations and functions.

5. Sports

"I see a large stadium in the distance," I observed. "Why is it located in the city center, which
you try to keep as small as possible?"

"Because it serves the entire city, and its
central location minimizes average user travel time
to and from it. Each satellite town center also has
a smaller stadium, but it is used for events which
attract local town residents solely or chiefly, for
instance, high school track events."

"I imagine that there have been notable changes
in sports since my time," I remarked. "Is American
football still popular?"

"Yes, there have been notable changes, and one
of them was the prohibition of football and all other
dangerous body-contact sports. Football caused so
many injuries and deaths that it was outlawed here
during the 21st century."

"But surely football gave a great deal of pleasure to millions of spectators each year," I protested. "And it taught discipline and team play."

'Yes it did," B4 said. "But, even in your day,
soccer gave as great or greater benefits at a far
lower cost in injuries and deaths. We have revised
the rules of soccer so as to make it much safer. Today, hard body contact in soccer is far less common
than in your time, and soccer is as popular in
America as football ever was."

"I infer that you have also outlawed boxing and
wrestling," I said.

"Yes, we consider them to be as brutal and bar-
barous as you considered bullfights and bear baiting.
Education and eugenics have made the average person

much less aggressive than he was in your time."

"Do professional athletes still earn top salaries," I asked.

"We have no professional athletes," she replied. "Education and eugenics have virtually eliminated the kind of men who would choose to devote the best years of their lives to athletics. Moreover, eugenics has drastically reduced the range of athletic ability. Our least athletic people are as physically sturdy and athletic as your average professional athlete. Since athletic prowess is now so common and uniform, it is much less admired."

"But surely sports give great pleasure to those who participate in them," I objected.

"Indeed they do," B4 said. "And that is one reason why there is far more widespread voluntary part-time participation in sports today than in your time. The major reason, however, is that almost all modern people are much more robust than your contempories. Men and women who have athletic ability enjoy sports much more than those who lack such ability. Moreover, the fact that physical strength is far more equally distributed also helps to make competitive sports more popular. For instance, few if any school children are now embarrassed or humiliated by their continual poor performance in school games."

"What are your favorite sports today?" I inquired.

"All sports have been changed more or less, but gymnastics, track and field events, tennis, badminton and other racquet games are still very popular. The average person—young or old, male or female—now devotes over an hour a day to one or more physically-demanding sports.

6. Space Travel

"In my time," I remarked, "mankind marvelled at the achievements of the first astronauts, and many futurists seriously predicted that men would eventually settle on other planets and even travel to distant stars. Science-fiction authors and scenario writers often described future trips among the stars. One of the most popular TV series was called Star Trek and was set in a giant interstellar space ship. Have these predictions come true?"

"Only to a very minor extent. All the planets have been thoroughly explored by means of unmanned space rockets, but only one planet, Mars, has been explored by man. There are several scientific

research stations in space and on the moon, with a
total staff of less than 10,000, but there are none
on any planet. We consider travel outside our solar
system to be quite impractical now and in the foreseeable future. Even if it were now possible to send
colonists to Mars or other planets, which it is not,
we would never do so because we believe the huge sums
required could be invested much more productively
here on earth."

"Have your science-fiction authors ceased to
write about interstellar space travel?"

"No, but they still write about witches, fairies,
and ghosts too. And those who write about travel
beyond the solar system are no longer treated as
scientific futurists. We distinguish between scientific futurism and science fiction far more sharply
and consistently than your contemporaries did."

7. Scientific Futurism

"In my time," I observed, "few men believed that
scientific prediction of future social events and
trends is possible. Many futurists wrote what they
called plausible scenarios, and most of those who
made firm predictions based them upon hopes and dog-
mas rather than upon scientific evidence. How did
futurism become scientific?"

"Over the years mankind gradually accumulated
far more complete and reliable data concerning past
long-run social trends likely to continue well into
the future. And historians learned how to conduct
research and write history in such a way as to help
futurists predict the future. It was also increas-
ingly recognized that periodic scientific public
opinion polls on proposed social reforms could help
greatly both to record and explain past historical
events and trends and to predict future major social
events and trends before they occur."

"But how can a public opinion poll reveal the
future?" I asked.

"No single public opinion poll can do so. But
if representative samples of people are polled on the
same question repeatedly over a long period of years,
the revealed growth of support for a proposed social
reform can be used to predict both continued growth
in such support and eventual adoption of the reform.

"For instance," B4 continued, "if Americans had
ben periodically polled on their attitude towards
slavery in the years 1750 to 1850, it would probably

have been possible both to predict the abolition of
slavery in the U.S. long before it occurred and to
achieve it more peacefully. Today we regularly poll
the peoples of all countries on many proposed social
reforms, and are therefore able to predict their
adoption many years in advance. Furthermore, such
polling greatly reduces final opposition to the adoption of popular social reforms because it makes their
eventual adoption seem reasonable and inevitable."

"But," I objected, "few laymen are competent to
make sound decisions on most social issues, and few
experts are competent outside their field."

"We know that," B4 answered, "but we also poll
experts separately on problems and trends within
their specialty. Moreover, in our highly educated
society, laymen have great respect for experts and
learn from them. Trends in lay public opinion lag
some years or decades behind trends in expert opinion, but they nearly always follow them. Moreover,
the fact that changes in expert opinion precede
changes in public opinion permits us to predict
social changes even earlier."

This was our last serious discussion of the day.
A few minutes later we returned to my room, where I
rested quietly until supper. After supper B4 gave me
another lesson in Voca by pointing to and naming
various organs of the body and objects in the room.
Then she rewarded me with a TV ballet performance,
but I fell asleep before it was over.

CHAPTER V

MY FIRST DRIVE THROUGH THE CITY

B4 returned the next morning soon after I had
breakfasted and undergone my daily medical examination. She was carrying a rolled map of Los Angeles
and environs, which she promptly unrolled and fasten-
ed on the wall next to the calendar.

"This will help to remind you each morning that
you are living in a new world, and will also enable
you to study the plan of the new Los Angeles. You
will note that the city center, where we are now, is
surrounded by a greenbelt and beyond that, by eight
isolated towns. My university is located in this
town—she pointed to one to the northwest—which
covers some of the area once occupied by old Hollywood. It is now named LA7. It is divided into
twelve villages, each of which has a village center
containing an elementary school, a supermarket, and
other facilities used only or largely by local village residents."

"How soon will I be able to leave the hospital
and observe the outside world more closely?" I asked.

"The doctor has just pronounced you fit for a
brief trip outside. We can leave at once if you
wish. However, to hide your identity, you had better
wear large dark glasses and a bandage on your head."

I assented eagerly, and within a few minutes we
were on the way to the hospital garage in the basement. There we seated ourselves in a small electric
cart very similar to those used on golf courses in
my day.

"I thought you did not allow the use of private
cars on city streets," I said.

"That's true," B4 replied, "but we do allow some
physically handicapped persons to have their electric
cars, and you still come under that classification.
You will not be a serious threat to pedestrians because this car has a top speed of 10 miles an hour."

We drove slowly out of the hospital basement
through the garden surrounding the hospital and
reached what B4 said was the main business street of
the city center of Los Angeles. It did not look like
old Broadway and Wilshire Boulevard. It was only
about half their width, and was lined on both sides
by rows of large old pepper trees. Song birds flit-
ted through their branches. There were no cars
parked at the curbs. Most of the busy traffic was

made up of pedestrians and cyclists. A slow-moving truck or two could be seen in the distance, but the street was remarkably quiet. Only bicycle noises and some talking by pedestrians could be heard. Beyond the sidewalk on each side there was over 20 feet of lawn, flowers, benches, and shrubs in front of each building, and even more garden space between large buildings. There were no small buildings, shops, or display windows. Apparently, all business was carried on by large firms in large buildings.

1. Retailing

"Why are there no show windows or window displays?" I asked.

"What are show windows?" she asked.

"Large glass windows displaying retail goods to passing pedestrians," I explained. "In my day many downtown streets were almost solidly lined with such displays."

"Of course," she remarked. "I had completely forgotten about them. They disappeared centuries ago. They wasted a great deal of heat, light, space, and labor, and the windows were costly and often broken. More important, perhaps, is the fact that we spend no money on competitive sales effort. We encourage people to save their money, not to spend it on luxuries. Finally, every home has a set of retail catalogs which picture, describe, and price nearly all retail goods."

"Where are the stores?" I asked.

"There is but one non-food store, a large department store, in each city or town center," B4 replied. "It is the large pink building on the right in the next block. It sells mostly goods not sold in town stores. We have learned that monopoly is far more efficient than competition. It yields many advantages of large-scale operation. Since each store is a monopoly, it makes no effort to increase its sales by personal salesmanship or advertising. And since each producer of retail goods is also a monopolist, there are no unnecessary style changes designed to cause forced obsolescence. By simplification and standardization, our monopolies have vastly reduced the number of models and styles of retail goods. They produce no shoddy or harmful goods. Our retail stores stock less than 20% of the extreme variety of goods offered in your stores. This alone has permitted a great relative reduction in total retail space, and also in retailing and manufacturing costs."

"In my time," I remarked, "many women got a great deal of pleasure from 'shopping,' from visiting several competing stores looking for novelties and bargains. Haven't you eliminated a harmless major source of pleasure?"

"In our view," B4 explained, "we have eliminated a costly major waste of human time and energy. Most men and women have always wanted to find the products they needed as quickly and cheaply as possible Our system makes this possible, and saves billions of hours of time each year."

"But if you do not advertise,"I objected, "how can consumers know where to shop and what to buy?"

"Since each store is a local monopoly, there is no problem of where to shop, and catalogs, merchandise tags, and sales clerks give customers far more, and far more honest and useful, information than advertisements supplied in your era."

2. Monopoly

"Do you mean that every business firm in America is a monopoly?" I asked.

"Every firm is a monopoly in its area. For instance, in the city center, where we are now, there is only one hospital, one hotel, one department store, one food supermarket, etc. And the same situation exists in each town or village center within Los Angeles."

"But don't these monopolies compete with each other for choice sites in each business district?" I persisted.

"Not significantly. You see each business district was planned so that it would be large enough to provide space for all monopolies, and so that each would be ideally located. Only an ideal land-use plan can maximize social benefit, and such a plan determines a different ideal location for each business firm. Moreover, no planned city has grown, and no new firms have arisen to bid for land in old business districts."

"We used to believe that competition is the life of trade, that monopoly would stifle initiative," I resumed. "Where were we wrong?"

"You confused the effect of competition between workers with the effect of competition between firms. We strongly encourage and stimulate competition between individuals, who now have far more equal opportunities, but we gave up competition between firms

-59-

because it results in costly duplication of facilities and services, wasteful sales effort, dishonest advertising, unnecessary fluctuations in sales and employment, shoddy products, high repair costs, unneeded style cycles, and other economic wastes. For instance, we found it impossible to plan and build ideal cities in which competing firms are free to start up new stores and offices and close down old ones whenever they please. We have only to look at pictures of your business districts to see the waste and ugliness created by competition between business firms."

"If there is no competition among producers, what incentive do they have to produce new and/or better products, or to minimize the costs of production?" I enquired.

"Every business executive is evaluated annually, and his salary or rank is based upon such evaluations. Managers who introduce beneficial new products, improve old ones, or reduce production or marketing costs of old products receive higher evaluations and appropriate salary increases and/or promotions. As a result, every manager strives constantly to improve his firm's products and/or reduce production costs."

"But," I objected, "wouldn't it be much easier and more efficient to measure profits and losses per branch, plant, firm, etc., and base managers' salaries on such results, as was done in my time?"

"We consider such profits and losses as but one minor factor in evaluating managers. They are nearly always heavily influenced by causes other than the actions of managers; for instance, by changes in raw material costs, or in export demand, or in the weather."

3. Clothing

"I note that people on the street all wear very similar clothing, simple clothing much like our women's pant suits, tennis dresses, and Bermuda shorts," I said. "Is this a result of your standardization program?"

"There are custom tailors in all cities, and some women still make a hobby of dressmaking, but custom-made clothing is very expensive because wage rates are very high. The vast majority of men and women now prefer to wear durable, mass-produced standardized clothing and spend the savings on more satisfying goods like music, sports, travel, books, pictures, and so forth. In your day the purchase and display of expensive clothing was a means of conspicuous consumption or deception. It made obvious unusual wealth, or gave a false impression about it. Today, income differences are far less extreme, and people have much less desire to display their wealth. They cannot deceive their neighbors and friends by wearing expensive clothing because all wage rates and salary schedules are widely published, and all personal income data are open to the public."

"Do you mean that there are no style cycles in clothing?" I enquired.

"Yes, we believe that artificial style cycles raise production and marketing costs unduly, and also cause a great deal of planned obsolescence. We introduce new materials and styles only after prolonged testing has proved them to be superior and/or cheaper, and, once introduced, they usually continue in use indefinitely."

4. City Architecture and Transport

As we drove slowly along the slightly curved tree-lined boulevard, I was astonished and fascinated by the color, decorations, and style of the individual buildings. I had observed from the hospital roof garden that each building was set apart in its own green park and had a roof garden on its top, but, because of the many tall trees, I had been unable to see clearly the facade of any building. Now I could see that each building was a distinctive and colorful work of art, much more beautiful than a typical building in old Los Angeles. No building had a plain or ugly back or side wall. Many walls displayed large murals or mosaics, and all other wall space was painted in pastel shades. The colors were as fresh and clean as when newly painted, a condition possible only in a city virtually free of smoke and smog. And the architecture of each building on the street was in harmony or agreeable contrast with that of its neighbors.

As we proceeded, B4 named and described the various buildings we passed—the court house, the auditorium, an art museum, the university, the research library, etc. She explained that there was no railroad station or wholesale warehouse in the city center because their operations would cause unpleasant noise and traffic. All railroad freight and passenger stations were located in outer greenbelts, and warehouses were placed next to the freight stations so that freight could be transferred directly from freight cars to warehouses. From them, freight was delivered to retail stores and other consignees, largely by way of greenbelt freeways, without passing through the city center or any residental areas in satellite towns.

5. Bank Buildings and Bank Deposits

"In your description of the functions of the imposing buildings we just passed," I remarked, "you failed to call my attention to any bank buildings. In my day the most expensive and impressive structures in central business districts were bank buildings. Where are your handsome bank buildings?"

"We have no local banks, because we need no local commercial or savings banks," B4 replied.

"But surely people still need a local office to deposit savings and have checking accounts," I protested. "How do you provide such essential services?"

"All adults, and many older teenagers, have savings and/or personal checking accounts in our National Credit Bank (NCB), but this bank has only one large building, located in the city you called Denver, Colorado. All wage payments, pensions, and other personal income items are directly deposited by payors in personal checking accounts in this bank, and all debts or bills are sent directly to it, where they are immediately debited to the relevant checking accounts. Both credits and debits are reported monthly or quarterly, on standardized bank statements designed to facilitate both rapid comprehension by the depositor and easy crime detection by authorities. Nearly all of this debiting, crediting, and statement preparation and inspection is done by computers. As a result of such integration and automation, less than 1,000 bank employees in Denver are able to perform the work which required over a hundred thousand local bank employees in your time. Then the average U.S. bank check was handled by both payor and payee, and passed through two to six different banks and clearing houses. On average it cost over a dollar to write, mail, record, transport, and collect a check. The total national cost was probably over 100 billion 1980 dollars. We have reduced the cost per bank check by 90%, and have greatly improved the speed and accuracy of payment by check or check substitute."

"How do people obtain or deposit coins or currency?" I asked.

"Each city center has a money exchange office which accepts and pays out cash. And we still use many automatic teller machines. They can be found in or near all large stores. But coins and currency are little used. All large payments must be made by check."

"If there are no local banks, how do people obtain loans?" I asked.

"Every NCB depositor is allowed to overdraw his checking account by reasonable amounts until he has proven himself financially irresponsible. Then his overdraft privilege ends, and his debt is easily collected by deducting it from his income over a period of time. The National Credit Bank suffers no losses from bad checks or bad debts because all personal income passes through it, and every person has an adequate personal wage or pension income."

"Can local units of national monopolies obtain capital or loan funds in the same way?"

"No, they secure all the funds they use from regional or national offices of their monopoly, which is more aware of their needs than any outside bank could be. And each national trust or department obtains its capital from our National Investment Trust."

6. Bank Checks, Money, and Crime

"Why do you require that all large payments be made by check, and what is the limit on payment by cash," I inquired.

"We require that all payments above a minimum amount, now about $10 in 1980 buying power, be made by check in order to minimize crime and to help the police detect crime and catch and punish criminals. Payment by check or bank debit leaves a record which can be used by auditors, tax officials, police, and prosecutors to detect and demonstrate nearly all tax evasion, bribery, and other illegal use of significant sums of money. As a result, nearly all such crime was ended long ago without any increase in spending on law enforcement."

"But couldn't criminals accumulate large sums of cash and use them to bribe officials and/or escape taxes?" I asked.

"No, because no landlord, worker, store or other agency will accept cash, except for very small purchases," B4 explained. "Moreover, governments ceased printing paper money long ago, and it is very hard to carry, transport, hide, and count large sums of coined money. As a result, bank robberies and hold-ups virtually ceased. Stolen cash is difficult to carry and is almost unspendable. And banks contain no paper money."

"But aren't bank statements confidential?" I asked.

"Certainly not," B4 replied. "Soon after your time, governments began to require that all bank statements be submitted to regular police inspection. This became the chief method of crime prevention and detection before 2100 A.D.

"Surely, this was an immense and costly police function," I objected.

"No, because nearly all of the work is done by the bank computers used to prepare personal bank statements. They are programmed to call police attention to suspicious bank credits and debits, which are now so rare that police need personally inspect less than one bank statement in 10,000. Common knowledge of such review of bank statements is itself sufficient to prevent most misuse of demand deposits."

"Many of my contemporaries would have called widespread government inspection of bank statements an inexcusable invasion of personal privacy," I countered. "How would you answer them?"

"Some of those critics were themselves guilty of illegal conduct—tax evasion, bribery, crime, etc.—which they wished to hide from the government. Others placed their personal privacy above the welfare of the community. The protection of personal privacy is desirable when it involves no serious costs to other men, but it is socially harmful when it results in serious social costs. In your day, crime and corruption were rampant, and it was far more important to reduce them than to maintain the personal privacy which protected them."

Our street ended about half a mile from the hospital in a large parking lot and bus station on the edge of the wide greenbelt surrounding the city center.

"We could change here to a faster vehicle," said B4. "A bus leaves this station for each nearby satellite town center every two minutes, and they cover the two- to three-mile trip in about five minutes, But I think we should stay in our electric cart and take a separate bicycle path so you can observe recreational facilities in the greenbelt on our way to the nearest satellite town."

The greenbelt was about half a mile wide. The margin nearest the city center was heavily wooded. Then came a wide band of meadows and sport facilities —tennis courts, baseball fields, children's playgrounds, etc. Next came a forest band on each side of the banked and depressed freeway running through the center of the greenbelt. We passed over the freeway on a bridge used only by pedestrians, cyclists, horses, and electric carts. B4 explained that such paths never intersected with freeways or streets used by fast-moving vehicles.

When we reached the margin of the nearest satellite town, I noticed a very large garage and gasoline station with some private cars being serviced.

"I thought you allowed no cars in residential areas," I said. "What are these private cars doing here?"

"Some of them belong to residents of nearby areas," she replied, "but they cannot be driven into any city center or satellite town. They can be used only for freeway travel between towns and cities. Most residents rent cars for such trips, so few pleasure cars are owned by private persons."

7. Town and Street Names

B4 explained that we were entering Town LA6, and that, like other local satellite towns, it had a population of 40 to 60 thousand.

'Why is it named LA6?" Iasked.

"That name tells all truck driver, police, tourists, and others precisely where the town is located, i.e., almost due west of the Los Angeles city center. LA3 is due east, and LA5 due south of this city center. The same system of naming satellite towns is now used throughout the world. And streets are all numbered or lettered in sequence, so as to show their location in each town. Thus a tourist from any other city in the world can easily find his way around Los Angeles without a guide or map."

"But surely such use of numbers and symbols makes names less beautiful and charming, even if it speeds up delivery service and police response," I objected. "I would much rather live on Hermosa street in a town called Linda Vista."

"We do not object much to such street names, provided they are in alphabetic order on city maps; in other words, if Hermosa Street is between G street and I Street. However, such long names are used only

on local street signs, not on delivery addresses.
And most cities use single letters or numbers only.
We know that all savings made possible by efficient
methods of any kind permit men to earn higher incomes, which they can spend on more objects of beauty
if they please. It is just such efficiency throughout our economy which permits us to build cities so
much more beautiful than any of your age."

8. Satellite-Town Housing

We entered the nearest residential area of the
town and drove slowly down a curved, tree-lined
street. There was hardly any traffic because nearly
all the residents were still at work or school. We
passed one big, quiet, electric delivery truck. B4
explained that such trucks stopped at almost every
house on the street twice a day and delivered all
groceries and other retail goods except bulky furniture. Most residents, she said, ordered all groceries and other retail goods by phone or mail, and
visited retail stores only once or twice a month.
All dwellings had been partly furnished by the builders, so little furniture was ever moved from one
dwelling to another.
I noticed that nearly all the residential buildings were row houses or garden apartment buildings.
"You seem to have given up the old American
custom of living in separate detached houses," I commented.
"Yes," she replied. "The drastic depletion of
many natural resources has made it imperative to conserve land, fuel, and raw materials by living in
multi-family buildings. It is much cheaper to build,
heat, maintain, and provide utility services for
1,000,000 square feet of living space in row houses
or apartment buildings than in separate houses.
Moreover, families are smaller now, children spend
fewer hours at home, and more women are employed outside the home. Also, the elimination of street traffic and private cars makes apartment life much more
pleasant. And the concentration of population in
multi-family buildings facilitates the elimination of
private cars by reducing distances to and from jobs,
stores, and schools."
"Do individuals own their homes?" I queried.
"No, they rent them, but they are more secure in
their possession of them than were home owners in
your own day. They are guaranteed against unreasonable rent increases, and cannot be evicted except for

sound social reasons. Since our buildings are much
more durable than yours were, and since our cities do
not grow, it is rarely necessary to evict tenants in
order to tear down old buildings. Moreover, children
can inherit their parents' rental rights. For these
and other reasons, our housing turnover rates are far
lower than those for owner-occupied homes in your
century, and tenants take good care of their rented
homes."

"But why don't you permit home ownership?" I
asked. "Surely it would further increase pride in,
and care of, one's home."

"There are several good reasons. First, few
newly married couples can afford to buy a home.
Secondly, we do not want any family to acquire unearned wealth or suffer losses due to changes in land
values. Thirdly, we want to make it easy for workers
to move from one place to another without having to
sell one home and buy another. When such movement is
easy, labor becomes more mobile and wage-rate differences are minimized. Finally, we object to the
inheritance of real estate because this creates
unearned wealth for heirs, and makes the distribution
of wealth more unequal."

"How do you allocate housing units to individual
families?" I asked.

"We raise and lower the rent of each class of
housing units until demand balances supply. When two
or more families bid for the same vacant unit, the
high bidder secures it."

"But doesn't this policy discriminate unfairly
against low-income families?"

"The discrimination occurs when low incomes are
fixed, not when rents are determined. And, if personal incomes are properly determined, the effects
upon personal buying power, including rent-paying
capacity, are clearly intended and are socially
desirable."

I noted that the distance from the edge of town
to the town center was about a mile and a half, and
that the town center was encircled by a road perhaps
a mile long. In the town center was a large office
building which I was told housed the local export
business, in this case a regional division of the
national social insurance department employing a
local staff of about 14,000 persons. In addition,
the town center contained a department store, a medical clinic and hospital, a theater, an amusement
center, a junior college, and other facilities used by
residents of this town, but rarely by residents of

other towns.

B4 explained again that every town was planned and built as a single project and was designed so as to enable all residents to find work in it, to send their children to nearby schools, and to buy nearly all needed retail goods without leaving the town. The national government guaranteed the provision of enough jobs within each town to assure constant full employment for all town residents.

9. The Scale of Export-Plant Production

"But if everyone must live so close to his place of employment, how can you have factories large enough to enjoy the great advantages of large-scale production?" I asked.

"By specialization and monopoly," she replied. "Each satellite town has only one major export plant. We call a plant or office an export plant if most of its output is exported to other towns and cities. If a town occupies twelve square miles, it can easily house 40 to 60 thousand people within two miles of the town center, where the major export plant is commonly located. In a town of 60,000 the labor force is about 40,000, of whom some 20,000 can work in a single, major export plant which produces only one good. This permits a plant or office large enough to achieve over 90% of the maximum potential benefits of an optimum scale of production. We deliberately sacrifice the rest of such benefits in order to enable people to live in towns small enough to permit them to walk or cycle to their job, school, store, clinic, or the nearest greenbelt in less than ten minutes."

After this conversation B4 noted that we had better start home if we expected to reach there in time for lunch, and I readily assented for I was beginning to feel hungry. We returned by the same route we had come, and I silently marveled at the large numbers of colorfully dressed walkers, joggers, and cyclists on the quiet landscaped path. The greenbelt athletic fields were all full of active players.

"America seems to have become a nation of physical fitness addicts," I remarked.

"Healthy people enjoy games and exercise, B4 said. "And today's Americans are far more healthy and athletic than your contemporaries, primarily due to eugenic reform. Moreover, their hours of labor, 4 to 6 a day, are shorter, so they have much more time for sports."

"But aren't most adults at work at this time of day?" I asked.

"Only one shift is working now, and nearly all firms work two to four shifts a day," B4 replied, "so our sports facilities receive far more daytime working-day use than yours did."

When we reached the hospital, we went directly to the roofgarden cafe, where I had a delicious lunch of food I had never tasted before my rebirth. After lunch I resumed my interrogation of B4.

10. Religion

"In my time," I said, "one could not drive around Los Angeles as long as we have without seeing several imposing churches, but I have seen none. Has religion died out?"

"It has not died out, but it has declined and changed almost continuously since your day. Less than 20% of our adults belong to religious organizations, and most of them are more liberal than your own Unitarians. They hold their meetings in multi-use auditoriums and clubhouses in order to conserve their funds for activities more useful than the construction of church buildings."

"How do you account for such a drastic decline in religious faith?" I asked.

"Sociologists believe that the chief factor has been the steady rise in I.Q. due to eugenics. Even in your day the degree and intensity of religious belief varied inversely and markedly with intelligence, and we have raised the average I.Q. from 100 to about 200. Moreover, the continuous growth and improvement of education has also been an important factor. As in your time, every increase in the general level of education reduces the amount of religious faith. In the third place, the advance of applied science, especially medicine and psychiatry, has enabled political leaders and doctors to solve many personal problems for whose solution religious people once relied on prayer alone. Finally, the steady growth and continued success of scientific research has steaily increased popular respect for, and understanding of, scientific method. As a result, the great majority of men now perceive that this method alone is capable of discovering or creating factual truth, and that the alleged truths achieved by other methods are false or senseless. Philosophers puzzled for thousands of years over such problems as whether the universe is real or unreal,

-69-

ideal or material, finite or infinite, etc. Today it is generally accepted that such unscientific questions, and all answers to them, are literally senseless because it is impossible to conceive of any way to verify any answer by sensory observation. It makes no observable difference whether any answer is true or false."

"In view of these strong anti-religious trends, how do you explain the partial survival of religion?" I asked.

"There are still lonely or disappointed men who long for an unseen friend and comforter. There are still immature men who need a father figure to protect and guide them, or a mother figure to love them. And some men still find divine revelation a useful support for personal prejudices which cannot be based upon scientific research and observation. Also, a few men are religious because they were taught religion at their mother's knee and believe they honor their parents by professing religious opinions. Finally, we still have people who want to believe that they will live on or again after they have died."

"But don't men need religion to reduce their fear of death?" I asked.

"In our time very few people die before age 90," B4 replied, "and all dying persons are allowed and encouraged to avoid a painful death by taking sleeping pills. As a result, fear of death in old age has become rare."

11. Moral Values

"In my time," I remarked, "we already had many educated men and women who were not religious, but nearly all of them believed that personal conduct should be guided by moral or ethical principles, usually referred to as 'values'. Do your non-religious contemporaries still exalt such ethical theory?"

"No, they do not. They believe that nonscientific ethical theory is as useless and senseless as theology and metaphysics. It is as difficult for us to understand belief in ethics as it was for your generation to believe in witches. It seems to us that moral and ethical 'values' were no more than irrational personal or social prejudices which men tried to sanction or honor by calling them ethical values or value judgments."

"Do you mean that all our moral principles were false," I asked, in perplexity.

"We would not call them false," B4 said. "A principle cannot be false unless it is meaningful, and we now know that your moral rules were literally senseless."

"Senseless," I exploded,"surely you are exaggerating. The rule that 'stealing is immoral' is perfectly clear to me. It means that men should not steal."

"But why shouldn't they steal?" B4 asked.

"Because it is immoral and unethical," I replied.

"You are reasoning in a circle," B4 said. "I still do not know what the term _immoral_ means."

I paused for a moment to think this over, and then said, "The moral principle that stealing is immoral means that stealing injures the victims and society."

"But that interpretation reduces your moral principle to a mere application of social science. It is easy to prove scientifically that stealing and many other 'immoral acts' injure the performer and/or society. But this makes ethics superfluous. Moreover, your moralists did not believe that moral principles were mere applications of social science based upon scientific research. They believed that moral rules were based upon divine revelation or pure reason, and that men should be moral whether or not moral action is expedient."

"Yes, I believe you are right," I conceded. "But why are such moral principles senseless?"

"Because they are not based on sensory data, upon data obtained by means of observation. Indeed, it is impossible to conceive of any kind of sensory data or observation which could be used to prove or disprove the truth of any moral or ethical principle. All meaningful general statements can be so verified, at least in theory."

"You seem to imply," I resumed, "that a proposition is meaningless unless we know how to verify it."

"Precisely," B4 said. "For instance, the statement that the universe is ideal is quite senseless until we have learned how this claim can be proven or disproven."

"But you are now implying that all pure academic philosophy is or was senseless," I again objected, "because it consisted entirely of unverifiable propositions."

"Yes, we consider all such philosophy, apart from logic, to be senseless, and therefore useless. We rely entirely on scientific principles to guide both personal and social conduct. In your day, philosophy was the opium of the intellectuals, as one of your contemporary writers explained. It served only to confuse, obscure, and obstruct all efforts to solve intellectual problems."

"But if all ethical principles are senseless and therefore cannot be used to evaluate proposed personl acts and social policies, how do you determine which social policies and investments are desirable or beneficial?" I enquired.

"We try to measure and compare the total real benefits and costs of each policy or investment. We apply what your economists called felicific calculus, i.e., cost-benefit analysis. We believe that the sole function of government is to maximize net want satisfaction or welfare. Every social policy injures some people and benefits others. To maximize net want satisfaction, the state must measure and compare the pain and pleasure caused by each public policy. The only common denominator in which pain and pleasure can be measured and compared is money, so we try to give every citizen a chance to avoid any pain or secure any legal pleasure by paying money. The amount he is willing to pay for the marginal unit measures its pleasure or pain to him, and enables political leaders to adopt policies which maximize net want satisfaction and pleasure."

"But you provide many free goods," I objected.

"You are quite right," she answered. "But we carefully measure the costs of free goods, which permits voters or their agents to compare the costs and benefits of each class of free goods. Here choice is collective rather than individual, but the same kind of felicific calculus is involved. We never say that some goods or services should be provided or prohibited for moral reasons, or because men have natural rights."

"But," I again protested, "such reasoning implies that life itself has a monetary value, and even that it is proper to sacrifice a human life in order to save a sum of money greater than the value of that life. We considered life to be priceless, and the preservation of life to be a supreme moral end."

"Yes," she replied, "your statesmen and writers often made such claims. But their actions consistently violated their moral principles. They waged

war and executed criminals, often for allegedly moral
reasons. Moreover, nearly all of your economic activities resulted in predictable deaths due to accidents which could have been prevented by spending
more money on safety measures. Some of these deaths
should have been prevented because the cost of the
necessary safety measures was less than the value of
human life, but many preventable deaths should not
have been prevented because the cost would have been
greater than the value of the lives saved. Since men
are much richer today, the value of life is much
higher than in your time, and we therefore spend much
more to prevent accidental and criminal deaths, but
we still allow some deaths each year in most industries in order to save money, i.e., because the
saving is greater than the modern value of life. The
main difference between us and your contemporaries in
this matter is that we frankly admit that life, like
all other goods, has a value or price, i.e., that it
is not priceless."

"It almost seems that you have replaced social
ethics with welfare economics," I commented. "But
welfare economics cannot be used by individuals to
evaluate their own behavior. How do you induce individuals to behave so as to benefit society, or at
least not harm it?"

"We use a combination of economic rewards,
costs, legal penalties, and education. Our economic
system is designed so as to reward men for work,
thrift, good management, and other socially beneficial economic behavior and to make them pay, individ-
ually and collectively, for the goods they consume.
We also have a penal system which penalizes men for
performing illegal acts, and this system is so efficient that the great majority of serious offenders
are promptly caught and penalized.

"Our schools teach children that they should
obey the law, be kind to their parents and children,
assist their friends and neighbors, and perform all
other socially desirable acts because such conduct
will help them to make friends, win promotions, earn
more money, achieve good government, and attain other
desired ends. In sum, we teach them that it pays to
be good, honest, industrious, and law-abiding. This
principle was largely true in your time, but it is
more generally true today because we have much more
accurate and effective ways of observing, evaluating,
and rewarding or penalizing all personal behavior,
especially illegal behavior."

"But how do you persuade men to spend their time

and money doing good for other persons anonymously?"
I asked.

"We have discovered that most sincere 'do-good-
ers', as you called them, need no promise of reward
in this world or the next. They actually enjoy helping their fellow men, especially those most in need
of help. We believe you grossly depreciated and
degraded such men in your day by asserting that they
did good only or partly in order to obtain rewards in
heaven. Today, as in your day, those who work most
actively and unselfishly for social reform are less
religious than those who oppose such reform."

By this time I was feeling rather tired and I
suggested a return to my hospital bed. When we had
returned, I enjoyed a two-hour nap, and spent the
rest of the day studying Voca and listening to
concerts.

CHAPTER VI

A NEW LIFE FOR ME

The next morning, after my breakfast and medical
examination, B4 entered my room with two handsome
middle-aged men—I had yet to see any plain or homely
ones—whom she introduced as Dean P2 and Professor
OB. She explained again that only the first two
symbols were used to address people in conversation,
and added that both the Dean and the Professor came
from her university department and could speak my
kind of archaic English. Both had said "Good morning" and "I am most pleased to meet you" with an
accent much like that of B4's.

After they had seated themselves, Professor OB
enquired, "How are you feeling today?"

"I never felt better or more eager in my life,"
I replied. "I still think I'm dreaming, but it's the
most realistic and vivid dream I have ever had. I
hope I never wake up."

"Your feeling is understandable," said Professor
OB. "Your remarkable experience is almost as incredible to us as to you. We knew much about the 20th
century experiments in the preservation of frozen
human bodies. Indeed we still preserve some of these
bodies. But these radical and costly experiments
were discontinued after a few decades, and very few
of the frozen bodies were preserved in a frozen state
through the centuries. Most families eventually
became tired of paying the maintenance costs and most
endowments eventually became bankrupt. Moreover,
natural disasters, accidents, riots, strikes, and
other unusual events interrupted the supply of electricity and chemicals required to keep the bodies
frozen. Finally, although we are still trying, we
have as yet been unable to revive any other bodies
frozen after death. For these and other reasons you
are our first great success."

1. Plans for My Future

"You will therefore readily understand," he continued, "that our success in reviving you has received enormous publicity. If we had not carefully
protected you from visitors you would have been over-
whelmed by reporters, writers, photographers, television crews, and other persons. To protect you, we
have kept secret the location of the city and

hospital in which you are being treated, and we have published no photograph of you. That is why you have been able to move about the hospital and the city without attracting special attention. We plan to continue protecting you in this way for a year or two, both to hasten your integration and assimilation in our society and in order to facilitate serious study of your health, your behavior, your attitudes, and your knowledge. If you will cooperate, you can help our historians increase their knowledge of many important aspects of your age."

"I am most willing to cooperate," I replied. "I was a social scientist myself and I am fully aware of the significance of social change. Indeed, I specialized in studying the direction and rate of social change, and was a pioneer futurist. Moreover, I never enjoyed personal publicity, and would find it a great trial, even in this enlightened age. On the other hand, I have always enjoyed intimate scientific discussion with friends, colleagues, and students."

"That is just the sort of program we have plan-ned for you here," Dean P2 announced. "We would like to have you move from here to an apartment in a building on our campus reserved for university in-structors. You will receive the salary of a full professor and will eventually be listed in our cata-log as a senior research associate in 20th century history. You will not be required to give any lec-tures or to tutor any students."

"I was beginning to worry about my future life in your world, which is so strange to me. I have no friends or family and no trade or profession which would be of value here. I cannot even pay for the care you have already given me."

"Your worries are groundless," OB responded. "You are in fact an invaluable scientific asset. We spend hundreds of millions of dollars on historical research each year, and the information you can supply about your own age will be of very great value to us. In return for it, our historical research institute will be glad to pay you a salary for life. I am a research associate in this institute, and am taking notes on everything you report about the past. However, we wish to postpone systematic interrogation of you until you have fully recovered and have learn-ed to speak our language. I have reserved an apart-ment for you in my apartment building, which is lo-cated very close to the historical research insti-tute, which is part of a residential university loca-ted in a town on the western side of Los Angeles. Of

course, after you have learned our language, you will
be free to live and work wherever you wish. But I
think you will enjoy a stimulating life in our
academic town."

"In the beginning, only a very few members of our
faculty, namely those who question you, will be informed of your true history because we wish to help
preserve your privacy and your scientific productivity as long as is possible. Your medical committee
has reported that you are fit for moving, and your
apartment is ready. If you wish, you can move into
your apartment at once. You will find the apartment
fully equipped, even to a supply of clothing of your
size. You will have to wear large dark glasses and a
head bandage for some time in order to remain unrec-
ognized by the public.

2. My New Apartment

"I am most eager to accept the position and the
housing you offer," I answered. "I will be ready to
move in 20 minutes."

All three of my visitors smiled, and two departed.
B4 fitted me with a head bandage, and said she would
wait for me in the floor lobby. I dressed, and met
her there 12 minutes later. We went to the basement,
got into an electric cart, and drove slowly to a
garden apartment building on the university campus,
which was located in the town center of LA7, and
parked the cart in a small cycle-port. B4 said that I
could keep the cart for my personal use. No one
would question my use of it because I still looked
like a very weak invalid, by 26th century standards.

We climbed the steps to my second-floor one-
bedroom apartment, and B4 showed me where all the
furnishings were kept, and how the equipment operated. The TV set had a screen about six feet square
built into the wall. The living room radio set, the
TV set, and the domestic computor used the same high-
quality sound amplifiers. She explained that over 50
TV channels and over 100 radio programs were available at any hour of the day, and no two programs were
the same. She switched on the TV set and tuned in a
ballet performance in color. She said this particular channel offered ballet programs 24 hours a day.
Over a score of radio programs offered the best university lectures day and night, she continued. And
all new plays, operas, concerts, musical comedies,
moving pictures, and other visual entertainments were
offered on TV, without commercials, even before they

were produced on the legitimate stage. She explained that her apartment was just two doors from mine, that Professor OB's apartment was directly under mine, and that he wanted to join us for lunch. She then left me to inspect my apartment, rest, and meditate until lunch.

We had lunch in an open-air restaurant on top of a nearby university building. After we had eaten and were drinking a strange but pleasing tea, Professor OB raised the subject of my continued education.

"I think that your first priority should be learning our language, which we call Voca," he said.

"I agree completely," I replied. "I would like to resume my Voca lessons as soon as possible. Could we start now?"

"That is what I had in mind," OB said. "Let us return to my apartment, where I have some texts."

At this point B4 spoke up. "From now on I shall normally leave you to the care of OB in the afternoon, but I will be with you each morning as long as you need special attention."

"I cannot thank you enough for your charming and thoughtful care," I said. "I could not have had a more helpful guide to this strange new world."

After B4 left me, we walked around the rim of the roof-garden once or twice, and then went to OB's apartment. He led me into his study and began the following explanation.

3. Microprint Books and Book Publishing

"You will notice that I have very few full-size books and journals in my library, and if you examine their titles you will find that most of them are the kind I do not use in my work as an historian. Yet I have in this room as much printed matter as a typical small college library had in your day. It is all contained in those small filing cabinets." He point- at some handsome file cabinets beside his desk containing about 100 small file drawers of the kind used in library catalogs in my day.

"See for yourself," he said.

I opened the top drawer of one file and noted that it contained semi-transparent plastic cards resembling thick, stiff camera films.

"Each of those cards is an entire book in micro-print," he explained, "and each drawer contains about 400 cards. Thus I have at my immediate disposal about 40,000 volumes of scientific literature. These

microprint book cards cost no more than a color post-
card cost in your day. Our university library has
about 500,000,000 volumes, but they occupy less than
100,000 square feet of floor space. And any library
user can obtain a book as fast as you could find a
catalog card in one of your large libraries."
     "Where is your microprint viewer?" I asked.
     "It is under that black cover on my desk. It
can also be attached to one arm of my easy chair or
to the head of my couch, so that I can use it when
sitting in a comfortable chair or when lying down.
It is much smaller and much easier to use than the
bulky viewers you were accustomed to. As soon as you
have learned to read Voca, I will help you to build
up your own library of microprint books."
     "In your living room I saw several shelves of
ordinary, old-fashioned books," I remarked. "How do
you decide which books should be published in that
form?"
     "We publish most books for small children in
that form, also some fiction, travel guides, dictionaries, catalogs and other books which may have to be
used where no view finders are readily available.
Dictionaries and catalogs are so published because
one often wants to skip many pages, and some books
with colored pictures are so published because colored pictures do not reproduce well on microprint
cards. But over 95% of the books and journals used
chiefly by scholars and scientists are published only
in microprint form."
     "Who determines which books should be publish-
ed?" I enquired.
     "We have taken great pains to decentralize such
decision-making," OB explained, "because we wish to
preserve a very wide freedom of book publication and
a wide variety of published books. All books are
printed and marketed by national monopolies, but the
editorial review and approval for publication is done
by many independent publishing agencies. For instance, every university and professional association
has such a publishing agency. And all rejected
authors can have their rejected book manuscripts
published at their own expense."
     "In my day," I remarked, "it was extremely dif-
ficult for able but unknown authors to find a pub-
lisher. I know from my own experience that it took
many months, often several years, merely to submit a
book manuscript to all competing suitable publishers,
some of whom kept manuscripts for months before re-
jecting them. With so many local publishers, the

problem must be even greater today."

"No, we have a single national literary agency that will perform this function for any author. It knows which publishers are most interested in each class of manuscripts, and it often submits copies to several publishers simultaneously."

"I once published a rejected book manuscript myself," I said, "and I found that critics would not review it, and book stores would not stock it. Is this still true?"

"No, all new books receive appropriate space in our review journals, and must be stocked by book stores if they get good reviews. However, our reviewers often give very low ratings to self-published books. We guarantee every author a hearing or review, but not a high review rating."

"Book prices were high in my time, especially for serious non-fiction," I observed. "Have you been able to lower them, relative to other prices?"

"Yes, indeed. Microprint books cost over 90% less to produce than paper books. Moreover, book prices, like all other prices, are now based on marginal costs, which are especially low for books. The major real costs of book publication—the author's time, editorial review, typesetting, etc.—are one-time fixed costs which no longer affect book prices, so even full-size book prices are, relatively, far lower today than in your time."

"Who then pays these uncovered fixed costs?" I asked.

"Except in the case of low-rated self-published books, they are covered by the national government," OB explained. "This enables many more people to benefit from such costs without increasing them. Marginal buyers pay all the costs they cause. Here, as elsewhere, marginal-cost pricing increases social welfare without increasing fixed costs. The subsidies required to permit such pricing do not cause or measure any additional real cost; they merely redistribute the burden of this real cost so as to achieve optimum output and consumption."

"But how does a would-be author support himself while he is learning to write and/or writing his first book?" I queried. "Some young authors in my era spent two or three years writing their first publishable book."

"The North American Government grants 2,000 new five-year writing fellowships each year to the most promising recent college graduates. If one of them publishes a good book during this trial period, his or her fellowship is renewed for five years, and so on indefinitely. The costs of these fellowships are social overhead costs which never affect book prices."

After this discussion of books, OB handed me a textbook and began my language lesson by naming and pronouncing the 66 letters, each of which signified one sound only in the Voca language. We worked together most of the afternoon. He explained that constant, intensive study of a new language is far more effective than intermittent, brief-period study of the kind customary in my day. He predicted that with such intensive study, and daily conversation practice, I would become fluent in Voca within a few weeks because the grammar, spelling, and conjugation were all regular.

Towards the end of my first afternoon of study, he turned on the TV receiver and showed me a daily program devoted to teaching four-year-olds how to read. He suggested I use this and other similar education programs to hasten my mastery of Voca.

4. Higher Eduction

At the conclusion of the lesson we had a cup of tea, and then went for a short ride in my electric cart. We rode around the campus and the adjacent residential area, and then parked in a universty plaza so that I could observe the passing students.

OB said that almost everyone who worked at the university or anywhere else in this town center lived in the nearest residential area, so that they could walk or cycle to work in ten minutes or less.

"How old are your university students?" I asked.

"They are about the same age as your own undergraduates," he replied, "but they are all doing what was graduate work in your day. Nearly all of the still-needed courses taken by undergraduates in your time are now taken by students age 14 to 17 who attend local senior high schools in each town center. Our children start school and begin learning to read at age three and attend school for ten months of the year. Moreover, they have an average IQ of over 200 by your standard. As a result, they are nearly all able to complete what you called an enriched college education by their 17th birthday."

"But surely there has been a great increase in the amount of knowledge since my days," I objected. "Doesn't this make necessary a much longer period of education for professional workers?"

"We have largely avoided that by requiring all professional students and workers to specialize far more intensively within their profession. In your time, for instance, a medical student had to memorize the name and location of every bone and muscle in the body, and had to learn to diagnose and treat all common diseases before he ever began to specialize. And specialties were very broad, by our standards. Today, an eye doctor treats only one kind of eye disease, and he specializes in the eye from the day he enters medical school. He does not need to learn anything about the bones, muscles, or diseases of the arms, legs, or trunk."

"But don't you need generalists to make many decisions as to which specialist a patient should visit?" I queried.

"We have doctors who specialize in preliminary diagnosis, and this specialty requires a longer training and demands a higher IQ than others. But diagnosticians do not have to learn how to treat any disease, and the theory of medical treatment now makes up over 80% of all medical science. Even in your day general practitioners, so-called family doctors, were being gradually and belatedly denied surgical privileges. Today, no general diagnostician is allowed to treat any patient for anything a nurse could not handle in your time."

"If professional men and professional training are so specialized, how can one university provide so many specialized majors?" I asked.

"It cannot. We have many specialized universities which, like your military academies, train men only for one or more of the various specialities in a broad field like medical care or engineering. Since these specialized universities draw students from many different cities, they are not located in city centers. They are export enterprises and are therefore placed in town centers. But each city center contains a university which trains local students in elementary education, art, police work, accounting, nursing, and other professions and paraprofessions, for which there is a large local demand. Most of the students at these city universities live at home and cycle to and from the campus each day."

5. Food Preparation

We returned to our garden apartment building about suppertime, and OB invited me to dine with him.

He suggested that I watch him prepare our supper so I would know how to prepare my own. He explained that he was living alone temporarily. His children had grown up and left home years ago, and his wife was attending a convention in China.

His pantry was full of prepared food in attractive glass and ceramic containers which only needed to be heated in a micro-wave oven for a few minutes. His kitchen had no cooking stove. We ate out of the attractive containers to save the time and food waste involved in transferring food from container to dishes and in washing the dishes and glasses.

"We used food containers very extensively in my day," I observed. "But the production of them consumed enormous amounts of energy and scarce raw materials, and the disposal of empty containers was a great and growing problem. You apparently use far more, and more expensive containers. Doesn't this result in far greater costs of production and disposal?"

"You will notice," he said,"that our durable food containers are standardized. All food manufacturers and processors who pack their products in durable containers use standard returnable containers which are re-used many times, and rarely by the same plant. Moreover, most empty durable food containers fit snugly within the next larger size container. Thus it costs far less to manufacture, ship, collect, and re-distribute returnable containers than it would cost if we used your inefficient methods. And, by re-using durable food and drink containers many times, we conserve natural resources and greatly reduce the quantity of solid waste to be disposed of"

"Do you mean that you no longer use metal containers?" I asked.

"Yes. We abandoned the use of metal food and drink containers long ago because metal became much more expensive than glass and plastics, because glass and plastic containers do not corrode and can be re-used, and because the customer can see the contents of a glass container."

"But isn't it a terrible nuisance to have to clean and return all food and drink containers to the grocery store?" I asked.

"Nearly all our food is home delivered," OB answered, "and the trucks which deliver food pick up and return all re-usable containers. Of course, we are required to wash them, but they are designed to facilitate rapid washing in our dish-washing machines. None have narrow necks."

-83-

"We were using growing amounts of pre-cooked, store-bought food in my day," I said, "but the flavor was much inferior to that of home-cooked meals or meals purchased in good restaurants. I must say your pre-cooked food is much superior to that I am used to."

"It is to be expected that methods of mass food processing have greatly improved in 500 years," OB remarked. "Today few wives or husbands can prepare home meals as tasty as those they can buy in containers. Moreover, the vast majority of adults have better uses for their time. And the wages of restaurant workers are so high that most families prefer to eat the great majority of their meals at home."

"Many utopian writers of my time predicted that dining at home would give way to dining in communal rooms," I commented. "They believed that collective preparation and serving of meals would save much tiring household labor. Why were they wrong?"

"They were correct in their prediction that large-scale food preparation would save labor and reduce the burden of housekeeping, but they failed to realize tht such economies could be realized more fully in food factories than in communal kitchens. They also neglected the advantages of being able to eat at home with one's family at any time of the day or night. Furthermore, public dining halls are unused between meals, while domestic dining areas can be, and often are, used for other purposes between meals. Finally, by dining at home one saves the time and energy required to go to and from a restauant or communal dining hall."

By now the food had been heated and a table set. There was no linen on the table, and the napkins were of paper.

"Why have you given up the use of table linen?" I enquired.

"Because it is so much easier and cheaper to wipe off a table top than to place, remove, and launder a table cloth. And fancy paper napkins cost much less than the laundering of cloth napkins."

I had noticed that OB's well-stocked refrigerator and pantry contained no canned or bottled drinks, and that he served none.

"In my day," I remarked, "a meal like this would usually include a canned or bottled beverage—beer, wine, cola, lemonade, etc. Have you given up the consumption of such drinks?"

"We have a great variety of beverages, and I should have asked you to choose one, but all are produced and marketed in powdered or highly concentrated form in order to reduce storage and transport costs. We believe it is very uneconomic to produce, store, and ship products consisting 90% of water and the heavy containers needed for such products. And we have so improved our powdered and concentrated beverages that they are almost indistinguishable from the originals."

"Do you mean that you use powdered wine and beer?" I asked, incredulous.

"Indeed we do. And I can prepare a sample in less than a minute."

He opened a pantry door, withdrew two small paper bags, mixed the contents with cold water from a tap on the side of his refrigerator, and handed me two glasses, one of wine and one of beer. I sampled each and found it satisfying, though the flavor of each was new to me.

"Do you still drink tea and coffee?" I asked.

"We drink only decaffeinated tea and coffee. Our health experts long ago condemned caffein as a harmful, habit-forming drug. Nowadays caffein can be obtained only on a doctor's prescription, and is used mostly to relieve mild depression."

After we had completed our simple but delicious meal, OB placed the dirty containers, dishes, and other table utensils in an automatic dishwasher, and turned it on. Altogether he spent less than ten minutes in preparing our meal and cleaning up afterwards.

After these tasks had been completed, we returned to his study and settled down in comfortable chairs.

6. Shopping By Phone

"I have been told that you order your food by phone," I said, "and I am sure you have improved upon our system. Could you explain your system?"

OB walked to the shelf beside his telephone, picked up a large book and brought it to me. I opened it and found it resembled an old Sears Roebuck mail-order catalog.

"This catalog contains pictures and/or descriptions of all food products and beverages. Each size container of each product has a catalog number beginning with the first letter of the name of the product. To order any product by phone, you first dial the telephone number of the nearest grocery warehouse, and then dial the catalog number of each item you wish to order. Your order is automatically recorded and the ordered goods are automatically assembled in the warehouse. Such automation is economic because we have only one phone-order-taking grocery warehouse in each town. Moreover, such monopoly also radically reduces delivery costs. Each of our large electric delivery trucks has a crew of several men and serves every house or building on the street. At most stops, deliveries are made simultaneously to two, three, or four different houses or apartments. Normally, all orders submitted before noon are delivered that afternoon, and all phone orders placed between noon and 6 PM are delivered before 9 PM"

"Do you use the same system for ordering and delivering other retail goods?" I asked.

"Yes indeed. And our catalogs contain such full and honest descriptions and pictures of all retail goods that customers rarely consider it worthwhile to go to the store and look at staple goods before buying. Of course, radical standardization and simplification of retail goods have also helped to reduce the need for shopping in person. Our stores sell no shoddy or uneconomic goods, and we have no style cycles and no special sales events."

"But how do you handle unexpected price changes," I asked. Surely you must cut the price of a good when unpredictable factors increase the supply of it or reduce the cost of producing or importing it?"

"We publicize such unexpected price changes by announcing them on daily TV and radio programs for housekeepers, and by reporting them in our local newspapers."

"How can delivery men deliver goods when there is no one at home?" I asked.

"Some apartment houses have managers who can accept deliveries. Most row houses and detached houses have special outside containers for the receipt and protection of groceries delivered when no one is home. We have virtually no crime, so theft is not a problem. And the hours of labor are much shorter, so such food deliveries rarely remain unattended more than an hour or two. Finally, our delivery trucks operate at least 12 hours a day, every day of the week."

"In my day," I said, "housewives thought it necessary to visit grocery stores in person to select the best of the available meat, fruits, and vegetables. Isn't this still a good reason for shopping in person?"

"No, because fresh fruit and produce are now as
carefully and accurately graded as canned food. It
is no longer possible for a customer to pick out the
best steak or the best apples and leave inferior ones
for later shoppers. And prices are the same in all
stores in the same city.

"Moreover," OB continued, "shopping in person by
car was a major cause of street congestion, auto
accidents, and smog in your day. We learned long ago
that shopping by phone and home delivery of purchases
notably reduce congestion, smog, and auto use, and
also save a great deal of time for housekeepers."

7. Selling on Credit and Personal Identification

"In my day," I said, "many families did not have
a credit rating good enough to enable them to order
goods by phone on credit. And credit losses were a
major problem for all stores which sold on credit.
How have you solved these problems?"

"Today every family has an adequate income from
work or pensions. Every individual has a bank
account, and both his pay checks and bills due are
transmitted electronically to his bank. Thus no one
with money in the bank can refuse to pay any bill.
If any person runs up bills in excess of his ability
to pay, he is fined the first two times each year,
and thereafter he finds that his retail store credit
is restricted more sharply each time he overspends.
Since we have only one bank, and one chain of retail
stores in each city, and since we have a very efficient system of customer identification, it is relatively easy to combat overspending."

"What is your system of personal identification?" I asked.

"We really have two systems. Soon after his
birth every child has his name, i.e., his identification symbol, tattood on his inner thigh, and under
one armpit. The national government maintains a
personnel file listing all citizens by these numbers.
Thus we can immediately identify any lost child, any
victim of amnesia, any captured criminal, and almost
any corpse. But we rarely use these tattoos to identify customers.

"All persons old enough to buy goods or services
on credit have credit cards which are universally
valid. These cards display a clear identification
photograph, a signature, 3 fingerprints, a home
address, and other identification data. It is

extremely difficult for one person to use another's credit card. And, when he uses it to buy valuable goods, the goods are delivered to the address shown on the credit card."

"In my time," I said, "most Americans strongly opposed the use of domestic passports. It seems to me that your universal credit cards are virtually domestic passports."

'Indeed they are," OB replied, "but you used many credit cards, and it is obviously easier to use one universally-valid credit card than to carry several limited-use cards. The fact that your contemporaries disapproved of domestic passports but approved of credit cards shows that they were illogical."

"But," I objected, "even honest people can buy too many goods on the installment plan and become overloaded with installment payment debts."

"Our stores do not sell anything on the installment plan," OB said. "In order to both prevent such overspending and to increase the volume of national saving, the government requires that all purchases of consumer goods be financed by voluntary personal saving. We control total national personal income and the consumer price level so as to enable retail stores and other producers to sell their total output without advertising and without selling any goods on the installment plan. As a result, consumers cannot become overloaded with debt, and the large extra costs of installment selling are saved."

"But doesn't selling on credit resemble selling on the installment plan, and have similar effects?" I asked.

"It would if credit were extended for some period of time," OB explained. "In fact, all credit purchases are electronically debited to individual bank accounts on the day of purchase."

8. Sleep Learning

At this point I said that I was rather tired and thought I should return to my room. OB agreed, and walked to my apartment with me, carrying what looked like a small flat radio receiver. On the way he explained that it was a machine which would help me to learn Voca by playing an instructional tape while I was falling asleep or waking up, or even fully awake. He suggested that I place it on the table by my bed, and turn it on when I started to prepare for bed. It would then operate intermittently throughout

-88-

the night, and I could turn it off before leaving my
bedroom the next day. He promised me a new record
each week and assured me that use of the records
would markedly hasten my mastery of Voca.

After he had departed, I watched a superb nature
film on TV for a while before retiring and turning on
my sleep-teaching machine.

CHAPTER VII

A SCHOOL VISIT

When I woke up the next morning in my new apartment, I again felt lost because nothing in my room
seemed familiar. As my memory returned, I first
recalled awakening in a strange hospital, and then
the incredible realization of my belated resurrec-
tion. Had it all been a dream? Then, finally, I
remembered being brought to a new and strange apartment. Or was this a part of my dream? I quickly got
out of bed, inspected my new quarters, and found a
balcony. When I entered the balcony and viewed the
beautiful gardens and apartment buildings around me,
the smogless sky, and the quiet street, I realzed it
was not a dream. Reassured, I returned to my bedroom
and dressed quickly.

I had barely begun to investigate my new kitchen
when B4 arrived and immediately began to show me how
to find things and prepare breakfast. After breakfast she asked me what I would like to see today, and
I suggested an elementary school. We then walked to
my golf cart and set out for a village school. Again
I was deeply impressed by the handsome, landscaped
buildings on the tree-shaded streets, and by the
almost incredibly healthy and attractive people walking and cycling along the streets.

1. Educational Organization

On our way to the school we were to visit, B4
explained the geographical structure of the school
system.
"Each of our satellite towns (population 40 to
60 thousand) has a single central high school located
in the town center. Every town is divided into eight
to twelve relatively self-contained urban villages,
each just large enough to support an intermediate
school (ages 10 to 13). And every village is divided
into four to six distinct and slightly separated
communities, each just large enough to support an
elementary school (ages 5 to 9) whose pupils can walk
or cycle to school in less than five minutes. Every
community, in turn, is divided into several neighborhoods, each of which has a nursery school (ages 2 to
4), unless it is a neighborhood reserved for adults
without young children. A neighborhood is usually a
single garden apartment complex or square block of

row houses."

"Do you mean that the layout of satellite towns is based primarily on the needs of the school system?" I asked.

"Yes, I do," she answered. "The size of a satellite town is based on economic considerations, primarily on the size of the work force required by efficient export plants, but the size of each town unit—village, community, neighborhood—is based upon the needs of the school system. High-school students can travel safely much further than younger students; intermediate students than elementary pupils, and so on. Moreover, high schools should be much larger than intermediate schools, and so on, in order to provide more numerous and more specialized classes and teachers."

2. Elementary Education

We soon arrived at the nearest community elementary school, and we drove slowly around it once so that I could get an idea of its size and location before we entered it. I noted that the playground was spacious and displayed a great variety of athletic and recreational equipment.

"This school has about 100 pupils and is so planned that all the children who attend it can walk to school in less than five minutes, without crossing any street. The school playground is so well equipped and so near most homes that children use it throughout the day every day of the week. Playground supervisors are on duty every day until most children are in bed. As a result, little playground area is needed at home or nearer home, where the noise of children's play would disturb parents. By combining most private playground space into public playground space we have both reduced sharply the total area required for playgrounds and have also vastly increased the playground space and equipment available to each child throughout the day. At the same time, we have freed parents of most of the burden of supervising the play of their children and have improved the supervision of children at play. Our playground supervisors are all professionally trained and chosen for their special ability to handle children. And we have one playground supervisor for every 20 children."

"What is that big van parked on the school grounds?" I inquired.

"It is a mobile dental office. All children in

elementary schools receive medical and dental care in such clinics. As a result, parents rarely have to quit work or leave home in order to take their children to a doctor or a dentist."

"That should simplify the duties of parents," I remarked, "but don't many parents prefer to choose the doctors who treat their children?"

"Perhaps they did in your time. But our parents are intelligent enough to know that they are not competent to evaluate doctors or health-care treatments."

"Are all schools served by mobile clinics?" I asked.

"No, only those which are not located very close to town-center clinics. All our high schools are located near such large clinics. All children are required to receive regular routine medical and dental care while at school. This ensures full protection of all children with minimum inconvenience to both children and parents."

We now left the cart and entered the school. B4 led me to the office of the principal, F9, and introduced me as a visitor from a backward region of Siberia, where Voca had not yet been fully adopted. The principal took us on a guided tour of her school, and B4 translated her remarks to me.

I was immediately struck by the small size of the first class we visited. I could see only five children in the room.

"Is this a typical class?" I asked. "Do you have one teacher for each five children?"

The principal seemed surprised by my question. She did not know I was a visitor from another age.

"Our classes average about five pupils," she replied. "This is the usual number for elementary schools in North America."

I wanted to tell her that there had been over thirty pupils in my elementary school classes, but I realized she was unaware of my fantastic history so I said no more about class sizes.

"What are these curious machines the children are operating?" I asked, after I had seen them in several classrooms.

"They are the newest model multi-purpose teaching machines," the principal replied. "They can be used to teach nearly all elementary school classroom subjects except singing, speaking, acting, and composition."

"I saw two children sticking silver stamps in a small album," I said. "What role do those stamps play in their education?"

"We have a piece-rate incentive system to encourage children to study harder," B4 explained. "Every child is rewarded daily, sometimes even hourly, for completing certain lessons or for making a good grade on a test. In elementary schools we use silver stamps instead of money. Like your trading stamps, these school credit stamps are redeemable in goods. We have found that such rewards affect the behavior of school children as strongly as piece rates affect the output of adult workers."

"But don't the gifted children get the highest grades and earn all the prize money?" I asked.

"No, for two reasons," B4 replied. "First, there are three tracks or non-competing groups of school children, namely, the slow, the medium, and the fast. Each group is taught in different classes, and the number of stamps assigned to each group is the same. Secondly, most school work is divided into small bits or assignments, and the completion of each assignment is rewarded, however long it takes. Many of our teaching machines automatically issue a stamp or a coin whenever a series of correct answers has been given. As a result, our children are as eager to play with teaching machines as the gamblers of your day were to play the slot machines in Nevada. We have turned most dull school work into exciting play.

"Of course, in each track group the most able students do earn more than poorest, just as the most productive piece-rate workers earn more than the least productive, but in both our schools and factories the rewards of the least capable are generous. And inequality in school earnings prepares children to accept inequality in adult wage earnings."

"But suppose parents give their children allowances large enough to weaken or offset your incentives," I countered. "How do you deal with that?"

"Our parents have been taught in school the evils of such allowance policies. Nearly all of them therefore use a home incentive system. They base their children's allowances on work done at home. Moreover, many of the things children desire most can be bought only with school money."

"But don't such rewards increase the cost of education unduly?"

"In elementary schools the costs of piece-rate incentive systems are less than 4% of total costs. Small children respond to very small rewards, and their average learning rate rises by over 30%. For older children, higher rewards are necessary but they too result in very large savings in the total cost of education. Moreover, school earnings permit parents to reduce sharply the allowances they give their children. Our children learn to work for their money in school as well as at home. This teaches them the value of work and money long before they leave school."

"In my day," I said, "some critics complained that teachers' salaries seemed to have little if any relationship to the effectiveness of their teaching, but teachers' organizations strongly objected to teacher evaluation and incentive salary systems. Do you base teachers' salaries on their success as teachers?"

"Yes; we evaluate the work of all teachers annually, and base each year's salary on such evaluation ratings. Our most effective teachers earn salaries as much as 50% higher than those of the least effective teachers."

"But how do you measure teaching results?"

"We test all pupils twice a year, calculate the gain they have made during the previous period, and obtain an average gain for each teachers' students. A teacher's salary depends upon the average gain the students made during the previous period. We have found that the teachers most liked by their pupils and/or their principal are often not the most effective teachers."

In one of the classrooms I observed children viewing a moving picture showing Roman legionnaires fighting the barbarians.

"Why do you show commercial moving pictures during school hours?" I asked.

"We use commercial films with realistic historical sets and costumes to teach history. We find them more useful than textbooks in teaching students how men lived and worked in former times, and the children enjoy watching dramatic historical films much more than they enjoy reading textbooks. Of course, our teachers comment on each film afterward and help the children to understand the tools, the weapons, the customs, and the ideas illustrated in each moving picture. We also use many purely educational films to teach history, geography, and other subjects, from kindergarten through the university."

By the time we had finished touring the school building and its grounds it was noon and we went to the school cafeteria for lunch. B4 explained that the school system provided free hot lunches for all school children in order to assure a wholesome diet, reduce the burden of housekeeping, and make real incomes per person more equal.

"How do you prevent the children from eating candy and drinking sweet drinks which spoil their appetites?" I asked.

"We produce no candy," she replied, "and sweet drinks are not sold to children. We are able to prevent bootlegging because our people are law-abiding and because our banking system discloses to the authorities the source and the use of all personal income."

After lunch, F9 took us to the school gymnasium where a class of nine-year-old girls put on an exhibition for us. I marveled at their graceful mastery of difficult routines.

"These little girls perform like the high-school champions of my day," I remarked to B4. "Surely they must devote a large part of their lives to rigorous training."

After consulting with F9, B4 replied, "These children are the best gymnasts in this school but they are far from being local or national champions. They train only one hour a day."

"But how is it possible for amateurs to perform so well?" I asked.

"You must remember," B4 said, "that in our eugenic program we have bred for health and strength as well as for high IQ and good looks. As a result, an average child today is superior to your champion gymnasts in natural gymnastic talent. Moreover, we have learned far more about how to train gymnasts quickly and effectively."

3. Secondary Education

After the gymnastic exhibition, B4 and I said good-bye to the principal and walked to our electric cart. I had to return to the university for my daily Voca lesson, so we headed directly for home. On the way I began to ask some questions about secondary education.

"How many of your teenagers complete secondary school, and how long does it take?"

"Since our students advance more rapidly than yours did, they begin the study of your secondary-school subjects at a younger age, about 11 on the average, when they are almost halfway through our middle schools. As a result, our high schools are largely devoted to subjects taught in your colleges.

Nearly all of our youth graduate from high school, mostly at age 17, which means that they have completed what you called a college education by age 17."

"What are the chief differences between your secondary-school curriculum and ours?" I enquired.

"We place far more emphasis on vocational education than you did," B4 explained. "Every secondary-school graduate is required to have mastered a skilled trade or paraprofession, so that all are employable when they finish secondary school. Moreover, while doing advanced work in their vocation, they work two hours a day in a plant or office where they can practice the lessons learned during the previous week or two. We have found that vocational theories must be quickly and repeatedly practiced if they are to be properly understood and long remembered by students."

"But," I objected, "Doesn't this delay or weaken the professional training of doctors, lawyers, scientists, and other professionals?"

"No, we don't think so," she said. "We require potential professionals to learn marketable skills that will be of use to them. For instance, all high school students who want to become doctors must learn and practice some health-care skill like nursing, paramedical work, laboratory work, etc., and all potential lawyers must learn some paralegal specialty. As a result, all secondary-school graduates who fail to be admitted to medical and law schools are qualified for paramedical or paralegal workers."

"But how can high school students study both liberal arts and vocational courses at the same time? Even in my day, when the sum total of knowledge was much less, this seemed impossible."

"First, no high school student now needs to study a foreign language since nearly all the world speaks Voca. Secondly, our beginning high school students have already had some college-level courses in the liberal arts. Finally, all vocational courses are much more specialized than in your time. For instance, nurses and paramedics are trained to care for only one class of patients."

'How do you induce the right number of students in each city to enter each vocation?"

"We use extra monetary inducements to attract students to the less popular fields. Moreover, such vocations pay higher wages. Our general rule is to solve nearly all problems of control over people by using monetary rewards and penalties because this method gives individuals the greatest possible free-

dom of choice, and also makes physical coercion least
necessary."

"But surely you must have some minimum physical
and/or mental requirements for entering vocational
and professional careers."

"We do of course have such requirements, but
they are never anywhere near high enough to reduce
potential demand for any kind of job to the number of
openings. We know that personal desires and ambi-
tions greatly influence personal achievements, so we
try to give every young person a wide variety of
occupational choice. We have very sophisticated
vocational guidance tests which all students are required to take and to consider before they make their
vocational choices, but the final choice is always
left to the students, providing they can meet en-
trance requirements. You must also bear in mind that
today the average pay is almost the same in all
occupations."

This discussion was ended by our arrival at our
apartment building, where I had an afternoon appointment with Professor OB for a Voca lesson. B4 said
that she would call for me after breakfast in the
morning, and then we parted. I had lunch, and
proceeded to OB's apartment.

4.   Old Los Angeles

After our two-hour Voca lesson, OB turned on his
TV set. He said he wanted to show me an educational
program about Los Angeles in the late 20th century
and get my comments on it. The program resembled the
travel pictures of my day, but tried to give a much
more detailed picture of ordinary life. I had never
before seen a travel picture of my own home city. I
could not understand the travel lecture, but I did
notice several anomalous and inaccurate details, and
made notes on some of them. After the program had
ended, OB informed me that such films were used in
all history classes and asked for my comments on it.

"There were too many minor errors for me to
remember," I said, "But I can make some general comments. First, your actors are much too healthy and
handsome looking. Among your people I look like an
invalid, but I was envied for my good looks and
health by many of my contemporaries. If you want
your historical pictures to be accurate, you must
show the vast majority of people as fat, thin, tall,
short, homely, graceless, depressed, gross, vapid,
brutal, fearful, etc. Not one in a hundred of my

contemporaries was as handsome, graceful, cheerful, and intelligent looking as the typical actor in this program.

"Secondly, the views of downtown city streets were unrealistic because they showed too many handsome buildings and too much greenery. They failed to show all the ugly advertising signs, all the trash in the streets, all the old ugly vehicles, and all the overhead wires.

"Thirdly, your historical picture failed to make clear the enormous range of living conditions, from wealthy suburb to impoverished slums. Our wealthiest families lived in great luxury, but our poorest citizens lived in crowded, dirty, crime-ridden, run-down neighborhoods. I saw neither of these extremes in your picture, probably because it is hard for you to conceive of such inequality."

"Your comments are most instructive," said OB. "As soon as you can speak our language fluently, I shall introduce you to the director of this film so that you can go over it in detail with him. In fact, we can use your help to revise all of our historical films and books dealing with your time."

After our discussion of the film, I resumed my study of Voca, with his aid. The lesson continued to the time for supper, which he helped me prepare and shared with me.

5. TV and Radio Programs

After supper he gave me a lesson in how to use my radio and TV sets, which were quite different from those of my time. He began by giving me a 50-page monthly radio and TV program guide and explaining its contents.

"As you may know already," he said, "Our Los Angeles radio sets can receive over 100 different broadcasting stations, and our TV sets over 50 stations. Each station or channel is devoted to a single class of broadcasts and is named accordingly. For instance, the first channel on your TV control panel is marked with three letters which indicate the kind of programs carried continuously on that channel, in this case serious modern plays. The next channel carries only serious classical plays, and is marked accordingly. This system of program specialization and control panel symbols makes it much easier to find the kind of program you wish to hear without studying a program guide. Of course, the guide gives much additional useful information. It

gives the name of each program and the time it begins
and ends. It also rates each program."

"How do you determine program ratings?"

"We measure audience reactions at special limited trial program broadcasts, much as you did, but we
measure and report them separately for three classes
of viewers—high-brow, middle-brow, and low-brow."

"Does the government produce most or all radio
and TV programs?" I enquired.

"Certainly not," OB replied. "One of the most
important and widely accepted principles of government today is that nearly all means of propaganda—
the press, the pulpit, publishing, radio and television program creation and selection, etc.—should
be operated by competing private non-profit agencies.
We have tried to achieve maximum freedom of entry
into all creative and opinion-forming activities
because we wish to avoid control of such activities
by the government, or by a single sect or party.
The government owns all real estate used by the
media, but it leases facilities to many competing
users, most of which are consumers' or producers'
cooperatives, universities, school systems, churches,
etc."

"The production and broadcasting of radio and TV
progrms is very expensive," I remarked. "How do
co-ops raise the funds to meet these costs?"

"The national government appropriates each year
a large sum to cover these costs. The appropriated
funds are divided among the radio and TV co-ops
largely on the basis of the number of people who
listen to their programs. And co-op members provide
additional funds to support programs they are especially eager to produce and/or broadcast."

"Do you allow commercials?" I asked.

"We allow programs which consist entirely of
commercials paid for by advertisers, but we do not
allow commercials on educational or entertainment
programs. We believe commercial interruptions
greatly reduce the pleasure of listening to such
programs."

"In my time," I said, "free television programs
financed by commercials were being steadily replaced
by pay-television programs. Why did you abandon pay
TV?"

"Prices serve a useful economic function only
when they measure marginal costs or limit consumption
of scarce unreproducible goods. Once a TV program
has been produced and put on the air, additional consumption costs nothing. In other words, the marginal
cost of serving one more viewer is zero. Hence,

-99-

price should be zero. Charging a price reduces consumption and social welfare, but does not reduce
social costs. Moreover, the extra cost of transmit-
ting and receiving pay-TV programs, and of paying and
collecting pay-TV payments, are substantial. Therefore, pay-TV is grossly uneconomic."

"But," I countered, "isn't it unreasonable to
tax people to finance programs they do not listen
to?"

"Your government taxed people to pay for roads,
parks, museums, gardens, schools, etc., which some
people did not want or use. Moreover, today almost
everyone has both a radio and a TV set. And, if we
taxed only set owners, this would discourage unduly
the purchase and use of such sets. Only free provision of radio and TV programs can result in optimum
purchase and use of radio and TV receivers."

"Doesn't your decentralized competitive system
of program creation and broadcasting greatly increase
production and broadcasting costs?"

"Yes, it does, but that is the price of freedom
and variety of choice. We think the benefits are
much greater than the costs."

"How can your local program producers and broadcasters be free and independent when they must be
financed by regional or national agencies," I
enquired. "Don't those who finance free broadcasts
control the broadcasts?"

'No, because such financing is based entirely on
objective criteria, including the popularity of the
programs."

"Doesn't that rule out the production and broadcasting of unpopular programs?"

'It does restrict them," OB admitted,"but we
have many voluntary private artistic, scientific,
and political organizations which raise money from
their members and supporters to finance unpopular
artistic, scientific, and political programs."

After this discussion OB left, and I listened to
a light classical musical program until bedtime.
What a pleasure it was to hear no commercials!

CHAPTER VIII

ANOTHER SATELLITE TOWN

The next morning my charming guide and tutor, B4, arrived shortly after I had finished breakfast, and we set out in my electric cart for a nearby satellite research town. Its name, LA5, revealed that it was southwest of the city center. Traveling at about ten miles an hour we took about twenty minutes to reach our destination, the town center.

1. A Research Town

While we were driving through the greenbelt between the towns, I began to ask B4 some questions about the town we were approaching.

"What sort of research institute are we visiting?" I enquired.

"It is entirely devoted to research in medical statistics. All North American doctors are required to periodically ask 1% of their patients certain standard questions concerning diet, occupation, exercise, heredity, and so forth, and submit on standard forms both the answers to these questions and reports of all health-care treatments of those patients and their observed effects. As a result, this institute has the statistical data necessary to determine the correlation of the incidence and intensity of any disease or symptom with hundreds of possible casual factors. It also determines each year the efficacy of each drug or medical treatment used that year.

"You may recall that one of the greatest medical discoveries of your day was the discovery that cigarette smoking shortens the life of the average smoker by six or seven years. That momentous discovery was based upon the use of rather elementary statistics, and cost less than ten million dollars. We have never been able to achieve so important a discovery at so low a cost, but we still find the study of medical statistics to be very productive."

"How large is the institute we are to visit, and what does it specialize in?" I asked.

"It has about 15,000 workers, of whom about two thousand have both an M.D. degree in diagnostic medicine and a Ph.D. in statistics. It specializes in correlations between the consumption of individual foods and beverages and the incidence of individual diseases. Its most notable recent achievement was

the discovery that the consumption of synthetic lamb
varied inversely with the incidence of glaucoma among
persons over 65. It is expected that the application
of this new knowledge will reduce the number of glaucoma cases by about 2%."

"If the institute is so large," I commented, "it
must be the only export industry in this town."

"That is so. The town has a population of
around 50,000 and a labor force of about 30,000, half
of whom work in the institute. The other half are
employed in the stores, schools, clinics, government
agencies, and other enterprises that serve the local
population."

"But if you have only one export firm in a town,
and that so specialized, don't you restrict unduly
the vocational choices of town residents?" I asked.

"There is indeed some restriction, but even a
specialized research institute offers a wide variety
of vocational choices. It employs writers, typists,
secretaries, accountants, computer operators, personnel experts, purchasing agents, janitors, and many
other classes of workers. Moreover, the town stores,
schools, clinics, and other local firms offer a wide
variety of occupational choices."

By this time we had arrived at the town center.
The research institute occupied the largest and tallest building in the center. The building was perfectly round, and about 12 stories high. I noted
that it had no parking lots around it, only long rows
of covered bicycle racks.

After we had parked our car, B4 pointed to the
garden apartment buildings across the street and explained that all dwellings near the town center were
reserved for families with one or two members employed in the institute and other town-center firms.
There was hardly any motor traffic on the nearby
streets, only pedestrians, cyclists, and an occasional quiet electric truck or bus.

We entered the building and followed signs leading to the visitors' bureau. We had to wait about
ten minutes until the next tour of the building
began. Our uniformed guide then took us down one
long corridor after another. Nearly all rooms had a
one-way window on the corridor, so that we could
observe the interior and listen to the guide's talk
without disturbing the occupants. The most impressive room to me was one containing the centralized
computer bank. B4 explained that this computer
complex served many other firms in the city on a
shared-time basis, and that it worked most of the

night performing tasks assigned to it during the previous day. After we had completed our tour, we were invited to have lunch in the employees' cafeteria. When we had selected our food and found a table, I began to ask B4 some deferred questions.

"Are there many other towns whose chief export business is research and development?" I asked.

"Indeed there are. Most North American and European cities contain at least one town whose major export plant is a research institute. About 20% of our North American GNP is devoted to R and D. This share is much smaller in Asia and Africa because their per capita income is much lower, but the world average is about 15%."

"Apparently you spend far more of your national income on research, education, and health care than we did in my time," I said. "What do you spend much less on?"

"The items you mentioned now take about 40% of our national income, as compared with about 18% in your time, but we spend far smaller shares on private automobiles, defense, clothing, food, housing, and financial services. We have planned our cities so that few private cars are needed, and we have rationalized our economy so as to reduce radically the number of retail stores, salesmen, brokers, bankers, insurance and real estate agents, lawyers, gasoline stations, etc. And of course the standardization of goods and the automation of our factories have sharply reduced the relative cost of all manufactured goods."

After lunch we had to return home so I could take my Voca lesson. On the way back I asked a ques- which had been puzzling me for several days.

2. Hours of Labor

"What are the normal hours of labor now?" I enquired.

"As I explained earlier, the week now contains only five days. The workers in each work place, and on each shift, are allowed to determine democratically their own regular hours of labor, and to choose among shifts with different lengths and hours. We have found that most contemporary workers prefer a short working day to a short working week because the last hour of work each day is the most painful or the least pleasant. In North America the majority of workers now labor 4 to 6 hours a day, 4 days in our five-day week."

"Do those who work a short day or week receive the same pay as those who choose a long work-day or work-week?" I asked.

"No, indeed. All workers are paid according to the amount of work done, when output is measurable, and according to supervisors' evaluations and the number of hours worked, when output is not measurable. The workers know in advance how much wage income they will lose by voting for and securing a reduction in their hours of labor. They alone also know the personal benefit from additional leisure. That is why they should determine their hours of work. No supervisor can directly feel and compare the pain and pleasure due to a reduction in their work-day or work-week."

"But, if they have only one free day a week, how can they take trips or engage in other projects which require more than one day?"

"Nearly all workers work for large firms which can easily do without or replace any worker for a day or two. Thus we can allow nearly all workers to take off an extra day or two whenever they wish to do so. Moreover, it is now customary to take ten-day vacations four to six times a year, so the need for long weekends as travel opportunities is far less intense than in your time. And you must remember that nearly all jobs are more interesting and less tiring than then."

3. Number of Shifts

"How many shifts does the typical export plant or office work?" I enquired.

"The number of shifts depends largely upon the capital investment per worker, which is now far high-higher than in your day. The most highly mechanized plants operate four to five shifts a day. For instance, I know of an automobile factory with five shifts: 7 AM to 1 PM, 1 to 6 PM, 6 to 11, 11 to 3, and 3 to 7. On the other hand, many retail stores and offices with a relatively small investment per worker and a relatively small night-time customer demand operate only three or four shifts."

"But don't workers still dislike working night shifts?"

"They would object if the wage rates and shift lengths were the same day and night. But the economies made possible by night-time operation are so great that we can afford to, and do, pay much higher wage rates for night work. For instance, if an auto

-104-

plant operated only two day shifts of six hours each, it would have to be twice as large as one which produced the same output by operating 24 hours a day, and the investment in inventory and goods in process would also be far higher per worker. Thus every additional shift substantially reduces the need for capital by making capital facilities much more productive."

"But," I exclaimed, "doesn't multi-shift operation create serious difficulties for families or neighborhoods whose members work on two or more different shifts?"

"We have largely solved that problem by permitting all workers to choose the shift on which they work and by housing workers on the same shift in villages inhabited largely or entirely by fellow shift workers. This town has nine villages, two of which house workers on the first shift, two on the second shift, and so forth. The village schools, stores, and other service facilities have hours of operation most convenient for their residents."

4. Wage Differences

"You have told me that all students are able to secure any kind of vocational or professional education for which they are qualified, and that on graduation they are able to demand and secure any job for which they are qualified. It seems to me that under such conditions the demand for pleasant, interesting jobs, like those in research institutes, would be so great as to force their wage rates down well below those of unpleasant or boring jobs. Has that actually happened?" I asked.

"Of course. Lawyers, doctors, engineers, and other professional workers doing interesting, non-routine work receive lower wages than sewage plant workers, miners, and assembly-line workers. The firms which employ professional workers must amortize and repay the investment in their education, but the amortizatin payments go to professional schools, not to the graduates. In general, throughout the economy average earnings per occupation vary inversely with the relative demand for the jobs which produce them."

"But how do you persuade people to spend extra years in professional study? Don't they deserve a reward for such extra work and self-denial?"

"Our professional students enjoy study and university life. Moreover, all the costs of professional education, including living costs, are met by the

state and charged to future employers. Profesional
students are encouraged to marry and enjoy family
life while at the university, and they can afford to
do so. Thus, they do not make any sacrifices to
become professional workers. The full costs of professional education, including student living costs,
are paid by employers and passed on to consumers.
There is no need, therefore, to pay high salaries to
professional men in order to compensate them for any
personal sacrifice or for any private investment in
their education."

"How do you control the distribution of workers
among regions, cities, and towns?" I enquired.

"We use wage differentials for this purpose
also. Whenever too many workers seek jobs in any
occupation in any town, we lower the relevant wage
rate until supply and demand are in balance. As a
result of this policy, wage rates for all occupations
are below average in towns with the best climate and
environment, and above average in towns with the
worst climate. For instance, real wages along the
Southern California coast are about 15% below the
national average, while those in Kansas and Iowa are
about 10% above this average."

"How do you induce each worker to work well?"

"When individual output can be measured, we
measure it and pay very progressive piece rates. In
many other cases we measure group or shop output and
pay group piece rates. Moreover, all other workers
are evaluated by their supervisors at least twice a
year and their wages are based in part upon such
evaluations."

"Doesn't this result in excessive wage differences?" I objected. "In my day a great many social
reformers argued that large income differences create
social classes and class wars."

"We accepted most of that argument long ago, and
that is the chief reason we have abolished the inheritance of productive wealth. Moreover, about half of
all economic goods--medical care, education, child
care, etc.--are now provided free of charge. There-
for, if an executive earns twice as much as the
average worker, his gross personal real income
(including free goods) is only 50% above that of the
average worker. And we have found that, when all
workers in a shop are well-qualified for the work
they do, few if any piece-rate workers can produce
twice the output of the least productive worker."

"I am glad to learn that you have made personal
incomes far less unequal," I remarked. "But some of

my visionary contemporaries argued vigorously that personal incomes should be, and eventually would be, perfectly equal. For instance, they claimed that all significant wage differentials are unfair to children, who gain undeserved advantages, or suffer undeserved disadvantages, because of their parents' high or low incomes. How would you answer this argument?"

"We believe that by providing free and equal educational opportunities, child care, health care, school lunches and clothing, etc., and by making parental incomes much less unequal, we have gone far to answer this argument. Of course, the children of low-income parents still suffer some mild disadvantages, but the social advantages from the use of income incentives more than offset these remaining minor disadvantages."

5. Full Employment

"One of the greatest social problems of my era was unemployment," I remarked. "In most countries 20 to 50% of the potential work force was unemployed. In the 1970's, the decade when I was frozen, the official average U.S. unemployment rate was only about 6%, but the real rate, including all who would have sought work if suitable local work at good wages had been continuously offered them, was two to three times the official rate. And many backward countries had unemployment rates of over 40%. How have you achieved full employment?"

"We require that every plant or office in every city and town accept and give work to all suitable applicants within three to six months after receiving the application. But each plant or office fixes its own wage rates. When too many people apply for any kind of work, it lowers its wage rates enough to eliminate this surplus. It cannot deny employment to any qualified applicant, and it cannot discharge any competent worker, but it can easily control the size and make-up of its work-force by suitably varying its wage rates. Of course, our wage levels are so high that such wage cuts can cause no serious human suffering."

"Do you mean that labor unions have no part in wage-rate determination?"

"Precisely; our wage rates are determined entirely by local supply and demand."

"But each of your firms is a monopoly," I objected. "Doesn't this permit it to use its monopoly position to reduce wage rates and exploit its workers?"

'No, because all wage cuts must result in price
cuts, which benefit consumers, most of whom are
workers. Moreover, all monopoly profits accrue to
the state. No firm now has a motive to underpay or
exploit its workers."

"But how can business firms plan or budget their
operations when they do not know in advance how many
workers they must hire?" I asked.

"I will answer with a similar question. 'How
can a firm plan its operations when it does not know
how large its future sales will be?'"

"You imply that one is no harder to predict than
the other," I commented. "But surely two uncertain-
ties create more of a problem than one."

"Indeed they do. But if one should be eliminated, it would be much better to eliminate uncertainty
in demand. Every adult needs prompt and suitable
employment much more than he needs prompt provision
of any particular kind of economic product. Moreover, after the policy of accepting all suitable job
seekers had been in force for some years, the number
of new applicants for each kind of job declined
drastically and became far more predictable."

"One point still troubles me," I persisted.
"Couldn't any firm avoid or reduce its employment
obligation by declaring many workers unsuitable or
unemployable?"

"This was a problem in the beginning. It was
solved by authorizing the National Employment Service
to decide all disputed job-qualification cases. And,
of course, all firms were permitted and encouraged to
use piece-rate wage systems, which base wages on
individual output, a policy which strongly discour-
aged unsuitable job-applicants."

"In my day," I volunteered, "some futurists predicted that the advance of technology, especially
mechanization and automation, would soon cause heavy
and indefinitely growing unemployment in advanced
countries, regardless of any reduction in the hours
of labor. Why were they wrong?"

"They ignored the fact that the demand for real
income, or economic goods in total, is insatiable.
The demand for any specific necessity can be satiat-
ed, but it is impossible to produce all the costly
luxuries men want. Secondly, and more important,
they ignored the future effects on real costs and
employment of the steady decline in the supplies of
rich natural resources.

"When we read the predictions made by the pioneer futurists of your day we are struck by the para-
dox that some of them predicted ever-increasing unemployment due to mechanization and automation while
others predicted a long decline in real wages due to
the need to spend more and more hours of labor to
produce fuel and other minerals or mineral substi-
tues. How do you explain these conflicting predictions?" B4 asked.

"I fear that both predictions were made to serve
conflicting economic or political ends, with little
regard to the relevant data. I see now that both
preictions were greatly in error."

6. Mobility and Alienation

"In my time," I said, "the average American
family moved once every five years, which made it
difficult for people to keep in touch with relatives
and old friends, and made many adults and children
feel insecure and alienated. Sociologists blamed
some crime, juvenile delinquency, drug addiction,
alcoholism, and divorce on such feelings of insecur-
ity and alienation. Have you been able to reduce
such worker migration and alienation?"

"One of the major purposes of our method of city
planning is to create relatively self-sufficient and
stable urban towns, villages, and communities in
which the typical resident will spend nearly all of
his life among relatives, old friends, and familiar
faces and places. But, of course, city planning
alone can not achieve this result. It is also essential to assure that almost every local school or
university graduate can obtain a suitable job and
career opportunity in his home town. We achieve this
result by proper planning of vocational education in
each town. Almost every student is taught a trade or
profession which he can practice in his home town or
city, and the number trained in each vocation is controlled so that nearly all can obtain work in their
home town. Finally, local employers are required to
hire all suitable job applicants. As a result of all
of these measures, over 80% of all AMerican workers
now work in the town in which they were born, and the
feeling of alienation and its ill effects have been
reduced to a relatively minor level."

"But suppose a local export plant is unable to
sell its capacity output and must reduce its work
force," I countered. "Doesn't this cause unemployment and emigration of workers?"

"No, it does not. Our export plants are not
operated primarily to make a profit, but to provide
jobs and produce goods. When profits in any plant or
industry decline, expansion of the industry is curtailed, but existing plants rarely reduce their output. To maintain sales and output at capacity levels, they reduce prices and suffer losses, sometimes
heavy and growing losses, but these losses are more
than offset by profits in plants which cannot expand
to meet growing demand. Proper control of new
investment in each industry minimizes both losses and
profits without causing any unemployment. In those
rare cases in which it is economic to shut down an
export plant and convert it to a new use, we continue
wage payments to all workers idled temporarily by the
plant conversion, and we take pains to design the new
or converted plant so that it offers about the same
number and types of jobs. No one ever has to leave
his home town to find a suitable job unless he has
been trained for a very special kind of work, such as
diplomacy or a rare form of scientific research."
    "But don't many young people want to leave home
and seek fame and fortune elsewhere?" I protested.
    "Some do, of course, but not nearly as many as
in your day," he replied. "Our cities are large
enough to provide a very wide choice of jobs and
careers, and incomes vary little from job to job and
city to city. Moreover, the vast majority of men
prefer to marry and settle down amid their relatives
and childhood friends."

7. Job Boredom

    "In my time," I remarked, "workers who performed
routine, repetitive functions--typists, truckers,
miners, assembly-line workers, etc.--were increasing-
ly complaining that their work was monotonous, boring, and even mind-destroying. Since your eugenic
policies have made men far more intelligent and creative, I should think that routine work would arouse
far more resentment today. Have you been able to
solve this problem?"
    'No, it is a perennial problem, one that has
grown with increasing specialization. But we have
minimized job boredom in several ways. Over the
years we have found it much easier to automate monotonous work than to automate interesting work. Moreover, service industries which employ professional
and highly skilled workers and assign their other
workers more varied tasks have grown faster than

manufacturing, mining, and transport. The proportion
of professional and paraprofessional workers in our
workforce is therefore over twice as high as it was
in yours. Thirdly, the remaining monotonous work is
divided up more equally among workers. For instance,
most assembly-line workers spend only half of their
working day on the assembly line. The other half
they work as gardeners, repairmen, teachers, policemen, etc. And no office-machine operator or typist
devotes more than half of his workday to such repetitive work. We have found that regular changes from
monotonous to interesting work greatly reduce boredom
and also increase output per worker."

"But isn't much time wasted in such job transfers?" I asked.

"Yes, but the time so lost is only a minor frac-
tion of the time wasted in your day in traveling to
and from the job. And the physical act of moving
from one job to another in the middle of the workday
is as relaxing as a coffee break, and therefore elim-
inates the need for one such break in the work routine."

"Doesn't your system increase the cost of vocational education by requiring that many workers be
trained for two different trades?"

"It has indeed increased such costs but the
increase due to this factor alone has been small.
Assembly-line work is so simple and repetitive that
it has never required much vocational training. Of
course, the supplementary jobs usually do require
special vocational training, but we are convinced
that the benefits of daily job changes more than
compensate for this additional cost. For instance,
the added pleasure which our coal miners derive from
shifting to more interesting part-time work above
ground far more than offsets the cost of the job
transfer. And truck drivers enjoy marked physical
and psychological benefits from a midshift or mid-
week change in their work."

8. Cemeteries and Funerals

On our way home I remarked to B4 that I had yet
to observe a cemetery in the new Los Angeles.

"Do you bury everyone outside the city?" I
asked.

"Nearly all bodies are cremated today," she replied. "But those which are not cremated are buried
in garden cemeteries located in the outer greenbelt.
Only a few religious fundamentalists still want

cemetery burials, which are relatively very expensive."

"Do you have funerals and wakes for persons whose bodies are cremated?" I enquired.

"Wakes are very rare in advanced countrie. Formal funerals are less rare, but are not customary. Nonreligious memorial services are far more common. In many cases, small memorial services are held before death, so that the dying can hear the praise and say farewell to their friends. And some persons planning a dignified death by suicide call together their closest friends and relatives to witness and ease their final act."

"What proportion of Americans still believe in life after death?"

"Less than 10%. Life on earth is now so pleasant that there is little temptation to long for happiness in another workld. Moreover, the great growth of science, education, and eugenics has created a population most of whom find it hard to believe in life after death. To most of us, the phrase, 'life after death,' seems self-contradictory and therefore meaningless."

By this time we had reached home and parked our car in the basement of our apartment building. I went directly to Professor OB's apartment for my daily Voca lesson. I found to my delight that, due to my use of the sleep teaching machine and the simple grammar and vocabulary of Voca, I was already able to carry on a slow, simple conversation with OB. At the end of the lesson he complimented me on my progress, and predicted that in another week I would be able to read childrens' books and understand most TV programs. I was so stimulated that, after supper in my apartment, I turned on a TV lecture on history and tried hard to understand it. I failed, but I did understand occasional words and sentences, and I resolved to continue this effort every evening until I succeeded.

CHAPTER IX

A TRIP TO MT. WILSON

The next morning B4 arrived, as usual, shortly after I had finished my breakfast and asked me what I would like to do that morning.

"I have not yet been out of the city," I answered. "I would like to see something of the countryside."

"Do you have any special destination in mind?"

I thought for a moment, and then said, "I used to enjoy the trip to the top of Mt. Wilson, behind Pasadena, where there was a famous observatory in my day. It would give me a wonderful view over Pasadena and other nearby cities. Would it be convenient to go there?"

"Perfectly convenient," B4 replied. "We can reach there in less than an hour and return in ample time for your afternoon lesson."

1. Highway Travel

We drove my electric cart to the nearest car-rental agency, on the margin of the greenbelt surrounding the town, rented a small car, and entered the depressed parkway leading to the freeway running through the center of the greenbelt. After traveling on this inner freeway circle for a mile or two we turned onto one running through the greenbelt surrounding Los Angeles, which led us to the freeway to Pasadena and beyond. All of these freeways were divided four-lane highways, but none were congested. The traffic consisted largely of trucks and buses, and moved at about 45 miles an hour.

As soon as we reached the outer freeway, B4 took her hands off the steering wheel and began to study a strip map. The car pursued its path down the middle of the righthand lane without swerving.

"Do you have a new system of automatic steering?" i asked, surprised.

"Yes, every lane has a wire down the center of the lane and each car has an automatic steering device which uses this wire to control the car. Of course, if you want to leave the lane, you must take over control of the steering wheel."

"But how can you be sure your car will not hit the car ahead of you when it slows down or stops?"

"Oh, every car has a radar-controlled device which will slow down or stop the car whenever necessary, and also an automatic speed control device. As long as your car is on a freeway, you can relax completely. You need pay attention only when you wish to turn off the freeway you are on."

Our car ran much more quietly than any I had known.

"What kind of motor does this car have?" I asked.

"It has a small steam turbine engine which burns hydrogen. Our gas tank is a cylinder of hydrogen-permeated crystals. When we need more fuel, the empty cylinder is recharged or replaced by another cylinder."

"What is the source of such hydrogen?" I enquired.

"Nearly all of it is produced by the electrolysis of sea water with electricity from giant nuclear-fusion power plants."

"But isn't hydrogen highly flammable and dangerous for ordinary people to handle?"

"You are thinking of liquid hydrogen," she replied. "We use hydrogen absorbed in solid crystals, which is far safer and easier to use. And it is handled only by skilled workers. All cars like this are maintained and refueled by experts. Individuals rent them for trips but are not allowed to tamper with the engine or the fuel tank."

"What make and year model is this car?" I enquired.

"All our cars are the same make. They are all manufactured by the same trust, which produces only one style of each size car. According to the identification plate on the dashboard, this car was manufactured 31 years ago but no style change has occurred since then, so it is still the latest model."

"In my day," I commented, "annual model changes accounted for almost 10% of the cost of new cars, and these changes made repairs far more costly than they otherwise would have been. The savings from your drastic reduction in the number of model changes must be enormous."

"Indeed they are," B4 said. "One saving you have not mentioned is that such standardization permits re-use of nearly all parts in junked cars. In your day you had to pay junk yards to haul away junked cars. Today a junked 30-year-old car is worth about a quarter of its original price since most of the parts have many more years of wear in them or can easily be reconditioned. In order to save scarce metals and minimize repair costs, we build cars to last for 40 years on the average."

At this point I began to study the country-side. I could see few signs of agriculture, only recreational facilities separated by woods and narrow belts of fruit trees.

"Why are there no farms in this open country," I asked.

"In most other parts of North America there are wide spaces and very large farms between cities. Due to our fine climate, the local demand for urban living space is so high that all land is used for urban development and adjacent recreational facilities. California now has a population of over 80 million, largely confined to the coastline and to coastal valleys. Therefore, we can allow only a few miles of open space between cities, and all of this is used for recreation. Agricultural products are imported from inland valleys and more distant regions."

2. Agriculture

"But I thought I saw some small orchards and vineyards," I countered.

"Yes, you did, but their functions are primarily recreational and decorative. They are cared for by city gardeners, and all city residents are free to pick their fruit when it is ripe. The only restriction is that no person is allowed to pick more fruit than he can eat or carry home in a small bag. Orange trees are the most widely planted fruit trees in these recreational areas because the trees, the blossoms, and the fruit are all especially decorative, but park visitors can also find many grape vines, apricot trees, peach trees, loquat trees, lemon trees, and so forth. They are planted around all picnic grounds and along many paths and trails. We also allow city residents to plant small personal flower and vegetable gardens in these intercity areas, but they cannot sell any of their produce. They can garden for pleasure and home consumption only."

"Has the family farm survived in farming areas?" I asked.

"Only to a very limited extent. Over 90% of all farm products are now produced on giant, highly mechanized farms, each employing thousands of workers who live in luxurious farm villages, travel to and from the fields by bus or cycle, and work only four or five hours a day. In those seasons when little labor is needed on the land, they enjoy a vacation and/or work in farm-town offices and shops repairing and renovating farm tools, machines, and equipment, and town buildings and facilities. All farm workers are guaranteed year-round employment at high city wages. We have no transient seasonal farm workers, except high school and college students, many of whom enjoy a month or two in the fields each year. Less than 1% of the North American labor force is employed full time in agriculture."

"How can such a small labor force feed such a large population?" I asked.

"Even in your own day 1% of the American labor force produced over half of your food. But you still had millions of surplus small farmers farming inefficiently, usually on submarginal land. We have given good city jobs to all of those surplus farmers, and have more than trebled the productivity of the remaining farm workers. Moreover, the drastic curtailment of meat production has freed billions of pounds of animal feed for human consumption. Finally, we now produce very large quantities of synthetic foods manufactured from sawdust, coal, corn stalks, and other vegetable fibers, most of which were wasted in your day."

"Why do your farm workers live in villages?" I enquired.

"Because this permits farm families to enjoy most of the advantages of city life. In a farm village, every home has sewer service, hot and cold water indoors, piped-in heat, cable TV and computer service, electricity, gas, and other urban utility services. It is far cheaper to provide such services for village homes than for isolated farm homes. Moreover, all farm-village children can walk to nearby neighborhood schools and well-equipped playgrounds, and all adults can walk or cycle to nearby stores, clinics, and other service agencies. Finally, most people like to live near each other and enjoy village social activities."

"In my day," I remarked, "young people were leaving farms and villages in large numbers, attracted by the variety, excitement, and opportunities offered by city life. How do you keep young people in your farm villages?"

"We pay them wages high enough to secure and retain the desired numbers and classes of workers. Farm-village wages average over 10% above those of

comparable city workers. Some youths do leave their
native farm village, but they are replaced by city
youths attracted by the higher wages and other advantages of farm-village life."

3. Geographical Reconstruction

As we climbed the San Gabriel Mountains behind
Pasadena, I discovered that the lower levels had been
terraced and built upon, that the upper levels were
also terraced and were heavily forested, and that the
mountain range did not appear to be as tall as it had
been in my day.
"Have you terraced and landscaped all of the San
Gabriel Mountains?" I asked.
"The process had already begun in your day," B4
replied, "but we have carried it a great deal farther. Because of the ideal climate, living space near
the California coast has a high value, and since your
day, we have increased the productivity of earth-
moving equipment and methods over 500%. We have
therefore found it economic to reshape most of the
mountain ranges on or near the California coast.
What you see before you is only a small sample of our
geographical reconstruction. Since your time we have
more than doubled the usable, near-level land area
along the coast of California, chiefly by leveling
and terracing coastal hills and mountains. Most of
the earth moved in this process was pushed into the
ocean and used to create islands and/or to extend the
coastline into the sea, by several miles on the average. Soon I will take you to the coast, where you
can see more of the results of this vast project."
"It seems to me that the San Gabriel Mountains
are not as high as they used to be," I remarked.
"Your impression is correct. Their altitude is
now at least a thousand feet lower than in your time.
Some of the earth removed was used for terracing on
this side of the range, but most of it was used to
fill canyons on the other side. As our road ap-
proaches Mt. Wilson from the rear, you will soon be
able to see that there is now a wide forested plateau
atop the entire mountain range. It produces large
quantities of lumber, and also serves as a popular
recreation area."
"It appears to me that the timber line is much
lower on this side of the range, and that the trees
are much larger and more numerous than they used to
be," I said.
"That is because terracing of the mountain side

-117-

has created space for more trees and because we now
conserve for first use on these terraces nearly all
the rain water that used to run down the slopes,
causing frequent flooding in the valleys below.
Coastal valleys no longer need the rainwater once
collected by damming mountain streams. All the
water not needed for forests and residents in these
mountains is now directed to the once arid valleys on
the other side of this mountain range."

"In my day nature-lovers would have strongly
objected to such radical alteration of the landscape," I countered. "How have you appeased them?"

"We believe that geographical reconstruction
often makes the landscape more attractive. In any
case, there are still vast areas of awe-inspiring,
unaltered landscape in our inland states, in Canada,
Siberia, Greenland, and other regions where few
people wish to live. And air travel is so cheap
today that men find it much easier and much less
expensive to visit these areas today than it was in
your age."

4. The View from Mt. Wilson

When we arrivwed at the lowered crest of the
ridge where Mt. Wilson had once stood, we parked our
car and walked to a viewpoint overlooking the valley
below. The sun was shining in a cloudless sky and
the air was as clear as it had been before World War
II. I could even see Catalina Island, over forty
miles away. Below me each detail of the rebuilt cities of Arcadia and Pasadena were visible. I noted
that the general plan of each was much the same as
that of Los Angeles. It consisted of a distinct city
center about two miles in diameter surrounded by a
greenbelt and by six to ten greenbelted satellite
towns.

"What is the population of Pasadena today?" I
enquired.

"It has about half a million population. It is
little larger than that of the new Los Angeles."

"But in my time Los Angeles had over ten times
as many inhabitants as Pasadena," I said. "Why are
they now equal in population?"

"The modern city of Los Angeles occupies only a
small part of the area it occupied in your time.
Moreover, the modern city of Pasadena includes the
territories once occupied by Altadena, Sierra Madre,
and South Pasadena. All such small suburbs have been
eliminated or consolidated with larger cities, often

as satellite towns. We have found that a city must
have around half a million residents to be large
enough to provide all the advantages of city life,
and that every town must be planned and built as an
integral part of a large city."

"But why shouldn't Los Angeles serve as the city
center for all the surrounding suburban towns, as it
did in my day?" I objected.

"Because then it would take too long for suburban residents to reach the city center, and would also
require the creation and use of a costly freeway and/
or subway system to handle rapid transit between the
suburbs and the city center. In our planned cities
of 400 to 600 thousand, all residents can reach their
city center quickly and safely by bicycle or by bus,
and our intra-city roads and freeways can be narrow,
quiet, and uncongested. Moreover, in a decentralized
city of half a million, all residents can reach wide
greenbelts and/or the open country-side by walking or
cycling for ten minutes."

"I suppose this urban planning is chiefly
responsible for the virtual elimination of the smog
that filled this valley almost every day in my time,"
I remarked.

"Yes, our city planning has helped greatly to
diminish smog by reducing the use of private cars.
But we have also adopted other means of reducing air
pollution. We have replaced coal and oil-burning
power plants with nuclear and solar power plants and
we have required most other industrial plants to
reduce radically their air pollution. All industrial
air pollutors must now pay a substantial tax based
upon the amount of air pollution they cause. And,
since this area is especially subject to harmful
effects from air pollution, we have banned certain
polluting industries like oil refineries from it.
That is why you can again see Cataline Island from
here on most days of the year."

5. Fresh Water Supplies

"We used to worry about the future water supply
for this area," I said. "We were importing growing
quantities of fresh river water from the Colorado and
Sacramento rivers, and we did not know how long we
would be permitted to do so. How have you managed to
meet the greatly increased demand for fresh water?"

"We now obtain over 90% of our local fresh water
from Alaskan icebergs towed down the coast,
ocean water desalted with power generated by immense

nuclear power plants. We no longer import fresh
water from distant rivers. All of the water from the
Owen, Sacramento, and San Joaquin rivers is now used
in the Sacramento and San Joaquin valleys. Very
little of it even flows through San Francisco Bay,
most of which is now a freshwater lake. And all
Colorado River water is used and re-used again and
again in higher inland areas. The lower inland areas
once supplied with Colorado River water now use desalted sea water pumped from desalting plants on the
Gulf of California. Boulder Dam has ceased to gener-
ate power because no Colorado River water is allowed
to flow past it. A similar situation exists in all
arid, semi-arid, and/or densely populated areas.
Only a few rivers in arctic and tropical regions
still run down to the sea. Most of the water in the
great rivers of Canada and Siberia has been diverted
south for hundreds of miles to satisfy the demands of
a population living in temperate climates."

"Do you mean that the great Mississippi River,
the father of waters, no longer flows into the Gulf
of Mexico?" I asked, incredulous.

"Precisely! Much of it has been converted into
a ship canal, but all of the fresh water which used
to flow into the gulf is now diverted into irrigation
canals which carry its water throughout the semi-arid
western plains from the old Canadian border to Texas.
All cities on or near the Gulf of Mexico, including
New Orleans, now rely solely on desalted sea water.
Mississippi River water is entirely allocated to
inland areas with an elevation well above sea level.
The last few hundred miles of this river actually
serve as a canal carrying desalted sea water to
inland riverbank cities and counties."

"But if rivers no longer flow down to the sea,
how do you dispose of the millions of tons of urban
sewage and industrial waste products we used to dump
in our rivers?"

"We prohibited nearly all river pollution centuries ago. We require that every city or group of
nearby cities process their own waste products. Most
sewage is now converted into fertilizer or animal
feed, and most industrial wastes are salvaged or re-
claimed."

"In my time," I said, "the Mississippi River was
a very important means of freight movement. Have the
changes you reported ended its use as a major waterway?"

"No, but river boats must now pass through many
locks."

"Don't the locks use up a great deal of water?"

"Yes, but all water so used, and often much more, is pumped back up to the canal from which it was drawn."

6. Air Travel

It was now almost time for lunch, but we decided to walk in the forest on the new plateau behind the mountain for half an hour before entering the nearby resort cafeteria. When we returned, we were fortunate enough to obtain a window table with a view overlooking the valley below. For lunch I had synthetic beef, peas, and a strange vegetable I had never tasted before. B4 said it was a new variety of turnip.

While I was looking out over the valley below, it occurred to me that the number of aircraft flying over the valley was far smaller than in my day, in spite of the great increases in population and income per person.

"There seem to be very few aircraft visible from here," I noted. "Have you developed a new method of long-distance transportation?"

"All our main airports are located at least five miles outside the nearest city, and few airplanes are allowed to fly over urban areas. Since cities in this prime climatic zone are so numerous and so close together, all long-distance airports are located outside these coastal valleys. The main airport serving Pasadena and nearby cities is located in the desert valley to the north of this mountain range, and other airports serving this region are located on artificial islands in the nearby Pacific Ocean, where planes cannot disturb nearby residents."

"But doesn't it take too long for travellers and trucks to reach these remote airports?" I objected.

"We consider the peace and safety of the 20 million local urban residents much more important than saving travel time for a relatively small number of air travellers. The planes which used your urban airports disturbed and endangered residents for up to ten miles around. It was even necessary to soundproof many school buildings so that the children could hear the teachers talk, and planes occasionally crashed on school grounds. Moreover, your streets were so congested that it took most urban residents an hour or more to reach airports. On our uncongested freeways travel is much more rapid. The residents of Pasadena and Arcadia can now reach our Antelope

Valley International Airport more quickly than they
could reach the old Los Angeles International Airport
in your day. There is a tunnel through this mountain
range that permits direct access to our desert airport. You can see the freeway leading to it there
almost directly below us."

"In my day some airlanes and airports were
already becoming congested," I resumed, "and the
danger of air collisions, especially near airports,
was growing. The great rise in personal incomes
since then must have resulted in a vast increase in
both pasenger and freight air traffic. How have you
solved the problem of limited air space?"

"The use of ultra-fast underground trains has
been very helpful. We have also created a world airline monopoly and greatly increased the average size
of airplanes. In your day, because of competition,
two or more half-filled small planes often left the
same airport for the same destination at about the
same time. Our airline monopoly has eliminated all
such wasteful duplication of service. Most intercon-
tinental passenger planes now carry over one thousand
passengers on each flight. This increase in the size
of long-distance airplanes has permitted us to move
over five times as many passengers in half as many
planes, which has helped greatly to limit air congestion. Moreover, the mere increase in plane size
has cut real costs per passenger mile over 50%."

"I should have thought that your high incomes
and low air passenger and freight costs would have
caused much more than a five-fold increase in air
traffic," I objected.

"Tourist travel has of course grown far more
than five-fold, and air freight also. But most airline passengers in your day were businessmen and
salesmen. Improvement in the means of communication
and the elimination of small competing firms and
aggressive sales effort have reduced such business
travel by over 90%. Business deals are now made
almost entirely by television-telephone conversation
between executives, most often between executives
of the same trust. The elimination of frequent style
changes and the standardization of goods has also
reduced both the need for business travel and the
need for air-freight service. It is no longer necessary to cross-ship millions of repair parts because
each manufacturer uses unique parts in his unstand-
ardized products."

"In my time," I said, "some of the noisiest
planes flying over residential areas were small

-122-

private planes. Do you allow such noise pollution?"
    "Indeed not. We do not allow private planes to
fly over or near urban areas, except at very high
altitudes. This rule is designed both to prevent
noise pollution and to prevent private planes from
crashing in urban areas."

7. Police Planes and Crime

    "If private planes are not allowed to fly over
urban areas, what is that plane doing over Pasadena?"
I inquired, pointing at a clearly visible small, slow
plane.
    "That is a police plane. It contains a wide-
lens moving-picture camera which is constantly film-
ing all visible outdoor activities in the entire city
of Pasadena. Every motor vehicle has on its top a
license number which can be caught on sensitive pho-
tographic film by day or night. Thus the police
always have a record of most local outdoor movement
of vehicles and persons.
    "They also use heat detectors and a camera with
a heat-sensitive film which permits the detection and
location of many dangerous fires, even before they
become visible. And of course the pilots and observers in the planes discover some crimes and fires by
purely visual observation. They also aid police cars
on the ground in the pursuit of criminals."
    "But all your city streets are lined with
trees," I objected. "How can you observe a vehicle
or a criminal on a narrow tree-lined street?"
    "If you will look more carefully, you will note
that there are planned gaps in the trees about one
block apart. These enable the cameras and observers
in police planes to see any person or moving vehicle
at least once in each block it travels. Moreover, a
police plane can easily improve its view of any suspicious activities by moving nearer to them."
    "In any case," I continued, "I am surprised that
you have enough crime to justify constant air surveillance. Since everyone now has a job of his own
choosing, a good education, good health, a high I.Q.,
and economic security, why do people commit crimes?"
    "Crime has in fact been reduced by over 90%, but
it has not been eliminated. Some young people still
commit crimes to demonstrate bravery or boldness, or
to attract attention, and jealous wives and husbands
still occasionally kill their mates and/or their
lovers. Moreover, we now have laws against the use
of tobacco, hard liquor, and many drugs. Finally, we

still have a few criminal psychotics who are not
diagnosed and treated in time, or who relapse when on
parole."

"You explained that the police planes film all
outdoor activities, including many people who are not
criminals," I said. "What purpose does that serve?"

"It enables many executives to supervise the
work of their employees without being present. For
instance, the manager of a parcel delivery service
can request a print of the police film and use it to
determine whether any of his truck drivers or crews
took time off for a nap or a visit to a bar when
they were supposed to be working. And the chief of
police can similarly check on the movement of all
police cars."

8. Wild Animals

We returned to Los Angeles by a different road,
through what had been called the San Gabriel Canyon
but was now a wide, terraced mountain valley sloping
down to the top of the old, now filled, San Gabriel
Dam. Leaving this valley, we entered the freeway in
the middle of the wide greenbelt separating Pasadena
from Arcadia, the next city to the east. We passed
by an open-country zoo where many animals were feed-
ing in pastures. The sight of them reminded me of a
forgotten problem.

"In my day," I said, "animal lovers feared that
many wild species would soon become extinct. Yet I
see members of several once endangered species in the
zoo we are passing. How were you able to save them?"

"We were not able to save all of them. The
sperm whale, the African elephant, the tiger, the
grizzly bear, and many other species did become
extinct, but we were able to save many others by
domesticating them or by breeding them in zoos. Much
of the meat supply of Africa now comes from native
ruminants domesticated after your time, animals which
can live in areas unsuited for intensive agriculture
or European cattle."

"Do you still hunt and slaughter whales and por-
poises?" I enquired.

"Yes we do, but we are careful to maintain an
optimum size breeding stock. The World Federal Union
has ended international competition in whaling and
fishing. It carefully limits the total world and regional take of each kind of sea animal so as to
achieve optimum net long-run benefits from whaling
and fishing."

-124-

CHAPTER X

MORE URBAN SOCIOLOGY

When B4 came to pick me up the next morning, she
said that she had arranged to take me to see a criminal trial. As we drove to the courthouse in the
city center, she explained some of the legal proced-
ures which she thought might surprise or puzzle me.

1. Criminal Trials

"We do not have private lawyers who are hired by
individual litigants or defendants. All evidence is
collected and all arguments pro and con are prepared
and presented to the judge by professional employees
of the judicial system. Of course, all litigants are
permitted to speak for themselves. Thus our justice
is completely free. Our students can hardly believe
it when historians tell them that in former ages nonviolent defendants often had to spend months in jail
and/or many thousands of dollars to secure their
acquittal."
    "But," I objected, "any government is always
eager to secure a conviction. Doesn't your system
leave the innocent defendant unprotected or inade-
quately defended?"
    "No, because we do not reward prosecutors, in-
vestigators, or judges for securing convictions.
They are not allowed to become political candidates.
We train them and pay them to do justice. They are
as impartial as our judges. Since they have no
obligation to convict or defend, and cannot win votes
thereby, they collect only relevant evidence and use
only reasonable arguments. We have no juries, so all
evidence and argument must be of the sort which would
influence an experienced and specialized professional
judge or bank of judges."
    "But surely," I resumed, "some defendants are
far more articulate and logical than others. Doesn't
your system discriminate against the dull and inarticulate?"
    "Perhaps it does, though all court personnel are
taught and repeatedly reminded that they must take
active steps to minimize such discrimination. However, in your time, most of the dull and inarticulate
were poorer than other men, and thus usually had the
least capable lawyers. Your system of justice
greatly increased the advantages of clever and arti-

culate men by enabling them to hire the best lawyers."

By this time we had arrived in front of a handsome pink marble building surrounded by flower
gardens, which was our destination. We parked my
electric cart, entered the building, and looked for
the courtroom we sought. When we found and entered
it, I was surprised to observe that it was very
small, less than a quarter of the size of a courtroom
of my day. There was no jury box and no section for
spectators. We sat down in a row of seats directly
in front of the judge's bench.

"You will observe," she remarked, "that there
are no seats for spectators. For us a criminal trial
is almost as private and confidential as a medical
examination. We believe it is as inconsiderate and
cruel to publicize private crimes as to publicize
private ailments. Therefore, no spectators or
reporters are allowed to attend court trials. Newspapers report statistics on criminal convictions, but
are not allowed to print facts or rumors about individual trials or criminals."

At this point the judge, a very handsome middle-
aged woman named T7, walked in and seated herself
behind the bench. She wore no judicial gown, and no
one rose when she entered. She was followed by two
judicial assistants, one a young man and the other a
young woman, who seated themselves at a table in
front of her bench. The judge gaveled for attention,
and the trial began. She announced that this was the
trial of ST 9R X4, a young woman age 22, for shoplifting. One of the judicial assistants then began
to read a summary biography of the defendant, about
eight typewritten pages in all. He mentioned some
childhood family and school problems, one conviction
for persistent truancy, and two previous convictions
for shoplifting. At the conclusion of this case
history, the judge asked the defendant, a nervous
overweight blonde, if she wished to amend or correct
the case history. She replied in the negative. Then
the judge nodded to the other judicial assistant who
immediately began to read a detailed account of the
latest alleged shoplifting incident, which had
occurred only six days ago. Among other things, she
reported that the theft had been filmed by a con-
cealed camera and that the defendant had been followed outside the store and stopped by a store guard,
who found the stolen merchandise—an expensive lady's
watch and a pocket radio—in her handbag. The judge
then asked the defendant if she wished to speak in

her defense. The defendant said yes, and explained briefly that her last boy friend had recently abandoned her, that no one ever gave her any nice presents because she was fat, and that she longed for expensive things she saw every day but could not afford to buy.

After a few moments' consideration, the judge pronounced her guilty of shoplifting. The judge reminded the defendant that she had only been fined for her first two convictions but that this third conviction justified a more severe sentence. She therefore sentenced her to three years parole and a fine of $5,000, the fine to be paid at the rate of $100 a month. The judge ordered that during her parole the defendant should enter no retail store and should be required to take a lie-detector test on criminal behavior every three months. The judge then rose and left the courtroom. The entire trial had lasted less than one hour. It would have taken several days in my time.

B4 then informed me that she had arranged for me to visit the judge and question her immediately after the trial, so we rose and followed the judge into her chambers. She was standing beside her desk when we entered, and greeted us most cordially. Apparently she was an old friend of B4's. After being introduced, we sat down and B4 began to act as an interpretor. The judge was aware of my origin, still a closely guarded secret. She opened the conversation by expressing her great pleasure in being among the first to talk to the first revived American, and asked what I thought of the new America. I told her how astonished I had been by my revival in a strange and exciting world, and how pleased I was with the great social progress since my time. I then began to question her about the trial.

"In my day," I explained, "criminal trials for felonies usually lasted for days, weeks, or even months, and occupied the time of over a score of people—jurors, guards, lawyers, etc.—for the duration of the trial. I congratulate you on the great labor-saving you have achieved, and also on bringing the defendant to court so quickly. Our courts were so over-crowded and inefficient that most defendants had to wait for many months, often in jail, before they were tried. How long does the average defendant wait for a trial now?"

"I had forgotten how bad the administration of justice was in your age," Judge T7 replied. "Today nearly all trials begin within a week after the

alleged criminal has been arrested. And very few
trials last more than a day. We believe that justice
deferred is justice denied."

"And how many appeals do you allow?" I asked.

"We allow no appeals except on convictions for
major felonies, and then only one. However, all
court records are read and reviewed by higher judicial officials, who may correct, discipline, or discharge incompetent judges, and who may--but rarely
do--alter sentences. No criminal is ever freed
because of a technical error by a policeman, court
assistant, or judge."

"I was very surprised to note your consideration
of previous convictions before rendering your verdict," I remarked. "Our judges and juries were given
no information about previous arrests and convictions
before they pronounced defendants 'guilty' or 'innocent.' We feared that such information would influence verdicts and result in unjustified convictions."

"I have never understood that fear," the judge
said. "Whenever you visited a physician, he required
full information concerning previous illnesses because such information makes diagnosis easier and
more accurate. The same reasonining justifies full
information concerning previous convictions before
rendering a verdict. A defendant who has been previously convicted is much more likely to be guilty
than one who has never been convicted. We have ample
statistical evidence to support this scientific
principle, and we find it very useful."

2. The Penalties for Crime

"I was also surprised that you merely fined the
defendant, who had two previous convictions," I said.
"In my day she would have received a jail sentence."

"We no longer imprison nonviolent criminals,"
the judge explained. "Imprisonment is costly to
society and harmful to most criminals. In our society everyone who wants work can get it. It is much
more economic to require convicted nonviolent criminals to work and pay fines which compensate the
victims than to imprison them. Moreover, our parole
system is very efficient. No parole officer is
responsible for more than 20 parolees, and he can
require them to take a lie detector test or medical
examination whenever he wishes."

"But don't you send them to jail when they break
their parole?" I asked.

"No, we merely assess another fine. Wages are

-128-

now so high that parolees can afford to pay very frequent and very high fines. And they can always get a
suitable job. You denied work to millions of youths
and most exconvicts, and then sent them to jail when
they stole or robbed to support themselves or to
supplement their welfare benefits. We give everyone
the chance to do the kind of work he wants to do.
If, nevertheless, he resorts to crime, appropriate
penalties are swift and fairly sure, so they need not
be severe."

"Do you mean that you rely on economic penalties
rather than punishment and/or moral rehabilitation to
reform criminals?"

"Precisely," Judge T7 replied. "But of course
society must lift all men well above the poverty
level before it can impose and collect substantial
economic penalties from all criminals. In primitive
countries, physical punishment and mutilation were
once common legal penalties because governments
could not afford to maintain jails and prisons large
enough to hold all or most convicts. In capitalist
America, jails and prisons were used primarily because most criminals were too poor to be controlled
by economic penalties, but today we can rely largely
on economic penalties. Only murderers and chronic
violent criminals are imprisoned for long terms. And
they are imprisoned primarily to segregate them, not
to reform them. We still have little success in
reforming such criminals, although many eventually
outgrow their violent stages. Fortunately, our
eugenic programs have drastically reduced the proportion which is prone to violent crime."

"Are your prisons like ours?" I enquired.

"Certainly not," the judge said. "All our prisoners live in remote but comfortable work camps,
often located on otherwise unpopulated islands, where
they largely police themselves and do enough work to
cover all costs of camp construction, maintenance, and
operation. Our prisoners are not a burden on society, as yours were."

"How do your crime rates compare with ours?" I
asked.

"I thought you might ask that question when I
learned you would visit my court, so I did a little
historical research," the judge replied. "Apparently
crime statistics were very incomplete and unreliable
in your day because they were prepared by thousands
of independent and largely incompetent local police
forces. But our historians specializing in crimin-
ology estimate crudely that nearly all crime rates

have fallen over 90%. Of course, a very large part
of the decline in economic crimes has been due to the
drastic reduction in the use of money and to the
thorough simplification of our economic system. A
bank robber cannot spend much of the money he obtains, because no one will accept it, and our corpor-
ate finances are so simple that corruption and
embezzlement are far more difficult to conceal."

I decided to change the subject, and asked, "How
are judges appointed?"

"We all belong to the judicial service, a special division of what you called the civil service,
and are appointed by senior executives in this service. The head of the service is nominated by the
service itself and his appointment is confirmed by
the national legislature. This makes him independent
of the president and his staff, whose behavior judges
may have to review. It also assures that all judges
are chosen by professional colleagues who are competent to judge their qualifications. We have great
difficulty in understanding the arguments used in
your day to justify the election of judges by voters
or the appointment of judges by politicians dependent
on large campaign contributors."

"Do all judges receive the same professional
education?" I asked.

"Certainly not. Each judge is trained in one of
over a dozen specialties—patent law, copyright law,
theft law, tax law, inheritance law, business fraud,
etc.—and handles only cases within his or her field.
We do not believe that an expert in patent law is
competent to judge a case in tax evasion. Moreover,
such specialization enabled us to radically reduce
the cost of educating judges and judicial assistants."

3. Newspapers

At this point, B4 rose from her chair and said
that we were most grateful for the interview and the
privilege of visiting T7's court, but that it was
time to leave. I followed her example, and we were
soon in our electric cart crossing the central greenbelt on our way home.

After lunch and a brief rest I went to OB's
apartment for my daily two-hour Voca lesson. After
some work on grammar and vocabulary, OB gave me a
copy of the Los Angeles Daily News so that we could
read it together. It contained only four pages.

"Is this the only daily newspaper published in

Los Angeles?" I asked.

"Yes," he replied. "We consider it uneconomic to publish two or more papers in a city. We can see no good reason why two or more separate accounts of each local news event should be written and published. When we want two points of view on a single news event, which is rare, we send two reporters to the event and then combine their reports or print them side by side. Thus no reader has to buy two papers to get two reports on these events."

"But how can you print all the news of a large city in a four-page paper?" I asked. "In my time each of our two major Los Angeles papers printed 40 to 100 pages of news each weekday, and several times as many on Sunday."

"There are several reasons. First, all national and regional news is assembled and broadcast by national and regional radio-TV news agencies. City newspapers print only city news. Readers who want national news stories in print get them from national weekly news magazines like your Time magazine, and from national journals of opinion like your New Republic.

"Secondly, our city newspapers contain less than half a page of advertising, all concerning local entertainment events, sporting events, education events, TV and radio programs, etc. These ads make no effort to sell; they merely announce programs, dates, and times.

"Thirdly, our local papers contain no printed matter that should be in book form so it can be preserved and read again or by other people. Thus, they include no comics, fiction, book reviews, art criticism, recipes, and popular psychology. Such printed matter should not be thrown away with the daily news each day.

"Fourth, our newspapers do not report divorce trials, accidents, family quarrels, private parties, individual crimes, court trials, or any news stories that would embarrass some private individual.

"Finally, we have deliberately reduced the size of our daily papers in order to reduce drastically the amount of paper used, and thus conserve our forest resources, and in order to reduce litter and the cost of trash collection and treatment."

"It seems to me," I complained, "that you have removed from your newspapers all the stories which made newspapers interesting in my time. We loved to read about spicy divorce trials and sensational crimes."

"Readers are still interested in such stories,"
OB observed, "but they can find all they want in the
form of history, autobiography, and fiction available
in public libraries. We do not believe that the
sorrows and tragedies of living persons should be
reported in the newspapers as a means of public
entertainment. In this respect we grant far more
rights of privacy than were allowed in the 20th century."

"But then how can you object to fiction being
printed in newspapers?" I asked. "Surely fiction is
popular and harmless."

"It is a matter of cost," OB replied. "Many
newspaper subscribers do not have the time or desire
to read daily fiction installments. Moreover, it is
inefficient to set type for any fiction twice. We
print all fiction once, in book form, and make it
available to all readers. Books are much more durable than newspapers, and can be read by many persons
before being discarded. By eliminating fiction from
newspapers, we have reduced the size and cost of
newspapers without denying anyone the chance to read
fiction."

"Why don't you simply stop printing newspapers
and let the public get all their news from radio and
TV broadcasts, which cost much less than newspapers?"
I asked.

"Because we believe people need daily printed
guides to local radio and TV programs, legitimate
theaters, musical performances, political meetings,
and other local events. A newspaper is instantly and
continuously available for use as a guide to local
events, while a broadcast radio or TV guide program
cannot be constantly available."

4. Public Libraries

While we were having tea after my Voca lesson, I
suggested that we visit a public library, for I might
want to use it, and I assumed it would be quite
different from any I had used in my former life. OB
readily agreed, and immediately after tea we proceeded to the nearest town-center library.

"We have public libraries in every village
center as well as in every town center," OB informed
me. "I am taking you to a town-center library because it is much larger than any village-center
library."

As we approached the library, located next to
the town-center high school, I was struck again by

the scarcity of motor vehicles and the large number
of bicycles on the streets. We parked my electric
cart next to another, the only one there, and entered
the beautifully designed and landscaped library
building. OB took me first to a very large card
catalog, and pulled out a tray.

"You will notice," he said, "that most of the
cards in this tray are made of film. Each is really
a complete book called a microfiche. Any user can
remove it, take it to one of those copying machines
there, and obtain a near perfect copy for a small
fee, perhaps twenty cents in your money. Then he can
read it here on a viewing machine and/or take it home
to add to his personal library."

"How many microfiche books does this library
contain?"

"I do not know the exact number, but it probably
has several million. Microfiche books cost very
little to produce and occupy very little space."

"What are the paper catalog cards for?" I asked.

"They serve the same function as catalog cards
in your day. They list all full-size paper books
available here. We still publish some full-size
books because people often want to read in places
where no microfiche viewers are available, or where
use of a viewer would be awkward or tiring."

The card catalog seemed to separate the library
reading room into two halves, one looking much like a
library in my time, plus microfiche viewers on each
table, and the other looking more like a book store.
I remarked on this to OB.

"Yes," he said, "every public library includes a
book store. In fact there are no book stores apart
from our libraries. We learned long ago that most
library visitors are potential book-store customers,
and vice versa. Moreover, many book-store customers
like to use a library card catalog when selecting or
ordering new books, and many library users find it
convenient to be able to buy any book in the library
at the library. Finally, by having a loan library
next to each book-store we have substantially reduced
the sale of books readily available on loan."

"I assume," I remarked, "that the book store
deals only in full-size books, for you explained that
microprint copies of all local books are readily
available at minimum cost."

"The book store stocks only full-size books and
magazines, but it will order for you any microprint
book not available in the adjacent card catalog of
the public library."

"I was very fond of reading," I remarked, "and I spent many happy hours in libraries. One of my problems was to discover which books were most worthwhile or most suited to my taste. Book reviews were unreliable, and I could rarely remember their verdicts when in the library. Since the number of books is far greater today, this problem must be much more serious. How do you help readers select books?"

"We have gone far to solve that problem," OB answered. "All new books are read, classified, and graded by three or more expert critics before publication is approved, and the resulting classification and grades are marked on the spine of a full-size book or next to the title on a microfiche. All library catalog cards, publication announcements, book reviews, and bibliographies show these ratings, which take less space than the catalog number. Moreover, most nonfiction books contain a brief authoritative review of the book."

"But who would read a novel with the lowest quality rating?" I asked.

"Even in your time the best-selling novels received low quality ratings from most literary critics. A quality rating indicates the class of people who will enjoy a novel, and our critics and readers understand this. We do not publish books which we think very few readers will want or enjoy, except at the author's expense. Our quality ratings are designed to help highbrow, middlebrow, and lowbrow readers find quickly the kinds of novels, verse, and drama they enjoy reading."

After this visit to the library, we returned to OB's apartment, where I had dinner with him. After dinner I decided to question him about a new subject.

5. Sex and Marriage

"In my day," I began, "there was a vast amount of talk about a coming revolution in family life. Has there been any such revolution."

"The great revolution in family life occurred when people moved from the farm to the town or city, and started to practice birth control, so that both husbands and wives could work away from home. In advanced countries, most city families had already largely gone through this revolution in your day. It took another century or two for most families in backward countries to complete this revolution. No comparable revolution in family life has occurred since then. Of course, even in advanced countries

-134-

the urban family revolution was not quite complete in
your time, and some further minor changes took place.
For instance, the proportion of married women who
work outside the home continued to increase in all
capitalist states, and the proportion of very young
children (age 2-6) in nursery schools and kindergart-
en continued to grow, but such trends were already
old and well established in advanced states in your
day. No radical change such as the rise of communal
families or polygamy has occurred. The individual
family is still the basic social unit, the basic
sexual unit, and the basic child-care unit."

"Do you mean that there has been no radical
change in sexual behavior?" I enquired.

"The only great revolution in sexual behavior
occurred as a result of the adoption of birth control, which made it possible to separate sex for
pleasure from sex for procreation. This revolution
was already largely complete in California in your
time. It greatly increased the amount of pleasure
derived from sex, especially amoung childless young
people. It permitted childless trial marriage, and
much more frequent and satisfying sexual relations
among married couples with two children."

"But I recall a great increase in the number of
illegitimate children when teenagers began to
indulge in sex more freely," I countered. "How did
you overcome that evil?"

"By making birth-control information and facilities more easily available and by teaching all young
people how to prevent conception."

"How do you minimize promiscuity among teenagers?" I asked.

"Chiefly by encouraging and facilitating monogamous affairs. We have found that most teenagers,
like most adults, prefer monogamous to promiscuous
relationships when both are equally available. However, some teenage promiscuity is educational. We
have no laws against promiscuity and adultery at any
age."

"How does a teenage affair differ from a trial
marriage?" I asked.

"It is called an affair if the two parties live
apart, a trial marriage if they live together
but have done so for less than three years, and have no
children," OB informed me.

"Apparently, all your marriages are trial marriages initially. We were afraid that the adoption
of trial marriage would cause the divorce rate to
soar. Has this happened?"

-135-

"The divorce rate has risen, but not in areas like California, where it was high in your time. The high rate in California in the late 20th century proves that most Californians had already begun to practice trial marriage. The main change since then is that we are more honest. We now recognize and admit that all marriages are trial marriages, and we require all young newly-weds to postpone childbearing for about three yeas so that they will know they can live together in harmony before they start having children, but this is only a minor change. The great change is that California marriage customs as of 1980 have now spread throughout the entire world."

"In my time," I observed, "half of all California marriages ended in divorce. What is the divorce rate today?"

"It has fallen to about 30%, due chiefly to eugenic progress, the creation of full employmnt, and general use of computer dating. Moreover, the divorce rate among parents of children under 18 has fallen below 10%. The great majority of divorces occur before any children are conceived or after the youngest child has left home. Our parents give far more consideration to the welfare of their children than did your contemporaries."

"Is prostitution a serious problem in your society?"

"We still have some prostitution, but it is all voluntary and part-time. No man or woman has to become a prostitute to earn a good living, and earnings from prostitution cannot be deposited in banks and used to pay rent and other major costs of living. But prostitution is not illegal, and some women are occasional part-time prostitutes. They have an association in each city which is listed in the phone book. There is no street walking. And prostitutes must accept payment in gifts, or in money which cannot be used to make payments of more than $10. Moreover, competition from amateurs is stronger than in your time, and the relative equalization of personal income has also sharply reduced the effective demand for the services of prostitutes. Prostitution cannot flourish in a society where women earn as much as men, where there is no unemployment, and where the richest men earn less than twice the average income."

"In my day," I resumed, "almost 10% of American teenagers and adults were homosexual and they suffered from gross discrimination and many legal disabilities. How do you handle this problem today?"

"Our eugenic policies have reduced the proportion of born homosexuals by over 80% and our child-
rearing and sex-education programs have reduced the
proportion of conditioned homosexuals almost equally.
We do not regard homosexual conduct as wicked or
immoral, and there are no laws against it, but we
have tried with great success to reduce the number of
homosexuals because we know they are less happy and
productive than heterosexuals."

6. Computer Dating

"In my time," I observed, "one of the chief
causes of unhappy married life and divorce was the
hurried and unwise choice of mates. We believed that
marriage should be based on ardent love or infatuation, which was usually short-lived. Have you found
any way to make the choice of mates more rational?"
"Yes, indeed," OB answered. "We have developed
very sophisticated methods of helping every person
find a suitable mate and congenial friends. We have
developed what you called computer dating to a very
high degree, and nearly all individuals use it to
find mates and friends. Whenever a stranger comes to
live in this city, he is introduced by a city host or
hostess to precisely those people who are most likely
to be congenial with him and to enjoy his company."
"I recall hearing of computer dating in my
time," I said, "but most of the people who ran such
services were unqualified and/or dishonest. Moreover, most respectable people were far too proud or
sensitive to admit that they needed help in making
friends."
"We have made great progress in this field," OB
commented. "Our computer-dating system is managed by
reliable professional experts, is a monoply, serves a
large majority of the population, charges no fees,
uses very sophisticated methods, and has done a great
deal to omprove marriage and friendship. It is
especially helpful to widows, widowers, newly divorc-
ed persons, and young people who are living away from
home. Over half of all marriages today result from
dates first arranged by our computer-dating service."
"I ,well remember how difficult it was to find
congenial friends in a strange city," I said. "As a
university teacher and civil servant, I had to move
myself and family from one city to another three
times. My wife complained of loneliness after each
move, and my children suffered from the loss of their
friends. Sociologists often wrote and spoke about

what they called the problem of alienation."

"It was the rapid growth of cities which greatly intensified this problem in your century," OB remarked. "In a small town or farming district, the average resident knew nearly all of his neighbors and fellow townsmen, many of whom were relatives, and usually selected his mate and friends from among them. When he first moved to a large town or city, he knew hardly anyone. And any neighbor might move away before or soon after the newcomer became well acquainted with him. We have solved this problem in part by drastically reducing the average frequency of movement and by decentralizing our cities. Today most persons spend their lives in the town and neighborhood in which they were born. And they also receive throughout their lives professional assistance in finding congenial mates and friends. And we have learned enough about people to determine very successfully which kinds of people are most likely to be congenial."

"Do you use the same classification system and correlations in selecting possible mates as in selecting possible friends?" I asked.

"Yes, we believe that an ideal mate should have about the same qualitiies as an ideal friend of the opposite sex."

"But shouldn't a mate be much more sexually attractive than an ideal friend of the other sex?" I asked.

"Yes, but we have not learned how to measure sexual attraction in advance. We must therefore leave it up to the individual to select for sexual attraction. We merely give the individual a choice among a group of people, all of whom would be likely to become congenial friends after sexual ardor or infatuation has declined.. We are convinced that friendship is the ideal basis for marriage after the first year or two. And we have ample statistics to prove that marriages arranged through our mating service last much longer and are much happier than those which are based solely on emotion and impulse."

7. Feminism

This discussion of marriage reminded me of the active campaign for equal female rights, both in the home and in economic activities which had receved much publicity in the last decade of my old life. I decided to enquire about the activities of women in the new society.

"What percentage of professors and scientists are female," I asked.

"About 70%," OB informed me.

"In my day well over 90% of professors were male," I continued. "We thought male minds were superior to female minds, especially in creative scientific activities. Have you come to the opposite conclusion?"

"No, we have no evidence that female I.Q.s are higher than male I.Q.s. But even in your day there was ample evidence that girls read more books, studied harder, and earned higher grades than boys throughout their school career. Your universities were among the last great strongholds of obvious sex discrimination based on pure male conceit and self-interest. By physical constitution and emotional temperament, women are better suited than men to the quiet academic life. Men make better athletes, policemen, soldiers, and executives because they are bigger, stronger, and more aggressive, but women are better fitted for indoor academic work and laboratory research, and they enjoy it more than men. Moreover, the mere fact that men are better suited for and predominate in certain major fields—police, military, mining, agriculture, geology, etc.—implies that women must predominate in other fields. Finally, most women still function part time as mothers at home, and therefore need part-time jobs more than men. University teaching is an ideal field for part-time work since a professor can teach only one or two hours a day without any loss of efficiency or serious inconvenience to his students or his university superiors. In fact, part-time teaching is both less monotonous and more effective than full-time teaching."

"If women are better fitted for scientific research than men, why did they win so few Nobel Prizes and other research honors in the 20th century." I asked.

"Because they were taught from childhood that scientific work was a male activity, and because they were later denied equal educational and academic opportunities."

"But," I resumed, "doesn't your argument that women are better suited to study and academic life also suggest that most doctors and lawyers should be women, and can men tolerate female predominance in all these honored professions?"

My argument does suggest that, and in fact over two thirds of our doctors and most of our lawyers are

-139-

women," he replied. "In the case of medical care there are important, special reasons why the great majority of doctors are women. Most women are still modest enough to prefer to receive medical care from women. And nearly all small children fear women doctors less than male doctors. Also, doctors who are mothers can handle young children better than most male doctors can. Since women and children make up almost two thirds of all patients, these reasons alone justify a heavy predominance of women in medical work. Finally, women have smaller and more nimble fingers than men, an important advantage in most surgery."

"It seems there are fewer professional jobs for men than for women," I commented.

"Not really. Most engineers, contractors, agronomists, geologists, business executives, policemen, firemen, and military officers are still men. We merely distribute professinal work between the sexes more rationally than you did."

At this point I told OB I was feeling tired and thought I ought to return to my nearby apartment. When I reached home, I spent the rest of the evening viewing TV programs.

CHAPTER XI

SIGHTSEEING BY DIRIGIBLE

The next morning B4 arrived an hour earlier than usual, as planned, because she wanted to take me on a day-long airship sightseeing trip which left the local airport at 8 A.M. After a hurried breakfast together, we set out for the nearest town-center bus station, where we parked our car and took a fast freeway bus to the nearest airport. She explained that this local airport and the adjoining railroad freight yard served the nearest four garden cities and was about equally distant (six miles) from the center of each. AS we approached the airport she pointed to several large warehouse buildings close to the freight yard and airport and explained that they housed all wholesale distributors for the four nearest cities. All wholesale deliveries were made by quiet electric trucks moving largely over greenbelt freeways.

We arrived at the airport passenger terminal a few minutes early and I had a chance to observe the handsome people waiting there. I marveled again at the obvious good health and fine appearance of my new contemporaries.

Suddenly a loudspeaker announced that our sightseeing dirigible was ready for embarkation, and we walked out on the airfield to embark. The ship appeared to be about 400 feet long. I noticed that the passenger compartment was three stories high but very long and narrow. Each story was wider than the one below. We were ushered to outside seats at the front of the lowest level. B4 explained that she had bought the most expensive seats because she thought I would enjoy them more than other passengers. The floor of our level was transparent, and the seats were about five feet apart, so that I could look almost directly down, as well as sideways and ahead. There were only two columns of single seats, with an aisle between, on this lowest level, so everyone had an outside seat, but we alone could see ahead as well as sideways and down.

As soon as all the passengers—about 300—had embarked, the airship's motors began to hum very softly. Out takeoff was so gentle I was unaware of it until I noticed that the ground had fallen away below. The ship headed directly south, towards the

ocean. We passed over three garden cities, very similar in design to the new Los Angeles. Our altitude
was only about a thousand feet, so I could distinguish a great deal of detail in the scene below. I
was struck again by the prevalence of flower beds,
greenbelt trees, and meadows, and by the gay colors
of buildings. In about twenty minutes we reached the
ocean near old Long Beach. I was surprised to
observe a long flat island about four miles offshore.

1. The New Island Chain

"When was that island created?" I asked. "It
was not there in my time."
"It was begun over 300 years ago," B4 replied.
"This area has one of the finest climates in the
world, especially along the coast. After all land
along the coast was built up in planned garden
cities, the government decided to increase the amount
of such choice land by building artificial islands
along the coast. As the demand for such land
increased, the island chain was gradually extended
and widened. It now stretches from Santa Cruz to the
southern tip of lower California, and averages about
ten miles in width. Over 10,000,000 people now live
on this island chain."
"But where do they get their fresh water?" I
enquired.
"Most of it comes from fusion-powered desalina-
tion plants, but about a third comes from icebergs
moved here from the coast of Alaska. The icebergs
are melted in large deep drydocks, and their cooling
effect on ocean water largely offsets the warming
effect of nearby power plants."
By now our dirigible was over the island chain,
headed southeast. I could see that the island chain
below was covered by garden cities. The major intercity greenbelts carried wide canals connecting the
outer ocean with the inner bay.
"Where did you get all the rock and earth needed
to create these islands?" I asked.
"Some of it came from the nearby ocean floor,
but most of it came by barge from hills and mountains
which once bordered the ocean north of Los Angeles
and south of Tia Juana. All of the mountainous coast
south of Carmel has been excavated and terraced in
order both to provide more building sites along the
original coast and to provide the fill needed to
create an offshore island chain."
"If you had proposed such a reconstruction of

-142-

the California coast in my day, ecologists would have objected loudly and stubbornly," I said.

"Yes, I can understand that," B4 said. "The first stages of our earth reconstruction did have harmful ecological effects, but we soon learned to minimize and compensate for such effects. For instance, in your century the most universal and serious cause of ecological damage was the rapid growth in world population. We have not only ended this growth, but have reduced total world population by more than half from the high point reached in the 21st century. There are of course many more people living along the California coast, but there are far fewer living in the middle west. And the people living and working on this reconstructed coast cause no more ecological damage here than they would cause if they lived elsewhere."

"But haven't they driven away much of the shore fauna which used to live here?" I countered.

"Yes they have, but if they were to move inland they would drive away most of the land animals and game birds in whatever area they moved to. Moreover, the sheltered bays and lagoons behind this island chain contain large commercial fish, shellfish, and seal hatcheries and farms. And vast inland areas in North America have been depopulated and converted into game and bird refuges or reserves."

2. Other Coastal Reconstruction

Our airship continued silently and smoothly down the coast. As we passed Laguna Beach and San Clementi, where I had once lived, I noticed that the hills around these towns had been largely leveled and terraced, and that the earth and rock removed from them had been pushed into the sea in order to provide more building sites near the ocean. The terraces were designed and planted so that every building could have a virtually unobstructed ocean view. On the new hill crests behind the coast I could see a long, broken string of tall apartment buildings. The fortunate residents of these buildings had a fine ocean view on one side and an exciting valley and mountain view on the other side. I also saw an occasional tall building on the ocean front. B4 told me they were resort hotels, which could operate at capacity the year around because the local climate was ideal in both winter and summer.

"You will observe," B4 suggested, "that the construction of our island chain has prevented any waves

-143-

from reaching the old shoreline. As a result, ocean swimming is now far safer and more pleasant than it was in your time. Surfers can still find ocean waves on the outer island shores, and some of the beaches there have been carefully designed to produce ideal waves for surfers."

"I should think that the new protected bay or lagoon, I am not sure what to call it, would be too polluted for swimming," I objected.

"It is much less polluted than beach water was in your day. We no longer dump any human or commercial sewage into the ocean. It is all treated at its source and converted into fresh water, fertilizer, and useful raw materials. Even the rain water which flushes our city streets and cleans our buildings in winter is caught, treated, and added to our fresh water supplies."

At this moment I glimpsed a giant iceberg moving southeast. I noticed that it was pulled by two large tugs apparently connected by a cable which ran behind the iceberg. As we drew closer I saw that the cable spread out into a sort of wide tough fish net at the points where it touched the iceberg.

"Why doesn't the iceberg melt away before it reaches here?" I asked.

"Over 80% of the iceberg surface is under water, where the heat of the sun does not much affect it. Moreover, the speed of towage is calculated so as to limit melting to the optimum degree."

After we passed Laguna Beach the dirigible climbed slowly to about three thousand feet and I could see farther and farther inland. I observed that the rough hills and mountains which once covered the land behind San Clemente for some thirty miles back had been terraced near the shore and, behind it, had been leveled to create a vast plateau filled with garden cities and forested greenbelts.

"How in the world did you transform a rough mountainous area as large as that into a nearly level valley?" I asked.

"It took a long time, almost a century," B4 answered. "However, the labor cost of excavating and moving rock and earth is today less than 5% of what it was in your day. This should not surprise you, since this cost fell almost 80% in the hundred years before your hibernation began. We now have non-nuclear explosives a hundred times as powerful as any known in your time, and our giant excavators and earth movers are well over ten times as large as yours. Moreover, the long-run interest rate has

-144-

fallen to 3%, and level land in this climatic zone is far more valuable than land in most other regions."

"Have other countries reconstructed their coast-lines in a similar way?" I enquired.

"All coasts with a near ideal climate and a rich population have been so rebuilt, but they make up less than 10% of the world's coastal areas. For instance, many Mediterranian coasts have been so rebuilt, but very little of the coastal areas of Asia, Africa, and South America."

The speed of the dirigible had been gradually increasing ever since we reached the ocean and was above 100 miles per hour when we passed San Clemente, but I felt no vibration and very little motor noise. It seemed almost like floating on a cloud.

As we continued down the coast B4 pointed out a giant iceberg drydock where icebergs were melted by application of the waste steam and hot water from a nearby nuclear power plant and desalting combine.

When we reached San Diego, which was easily dis-tinguishable by its fine bay, our airship turned inland. San Diego itself had been as radically rebuilt as Los Angeles. It had become a complex of garden cities and intervening greenbelts, and the mountains behind it had been terraced and leveled for many miles.

3. Baja California

"Apparently this tour does not cover Baja Cali-fornia," I remarked. "Has Baja California been developed and reconstructed as much as Southern California?"

"Yes it has," B4 replied. "The merger of Mexico with Canada and the U.S. into the new state of North America, which occurred in 2091, soon raised the Mexican standard of living, i.e., real wages, to the U.S. level. Moreover, the climate of the Pacific Coast of Baja California is almost as fine as that of Southern California. As a result, the population of Baja California now exceeds fifteen million. To house this great increase in population, the Baja California coast has been reconstructed in the same way as the coast of Southern California."

"What are the main industries in Baja Californ-ia?" I enquired.

"Since the coastal climate is ideal, tourist hotels and other tourist facilities are a major industry. Research and development is probably the next most important industry. There are also many

electronic plants. And marine agriculture and sea
mammal production are important in what you called
the Gulf of California."

4. Desert Agriculture

     By this time it was twelve o'clock, and a stew-
ard brought us a lunch and placed it on a removable
tray before each of us. Soon we reached the edge of
Imperial Valley, the hot irrigated desert valley
which had supplied a large part of the California
vegetable crop in my time. It looked as green and
well-cared for as ever, but much of the land seemed
to be covered by enormous greenhouses.
     "What are those glass buildings used for?" I
asked.
     "They are used for soilless or hydroponic agri-
culture," she replied. "Many varieties of vegetables
are grown in them, using only sand, water, chemical
fertilizers, and sunlight."
     "But there seems to be ample desert land," I
objected. "Why not grow them in the soil?"
     "Hydroponic agriculture requires less than one
quarter as much water and fertilizer. All the water
and fertilizer not absorbed by one crop can be saved
and used by the next. Very little of the water evap-
orates and escapes, and none of it is lost in the
soil. And the water thus conserved contains in
solution all the unused fertilizer."
     I looked for the famous open canal which used
to carry Colorado River water to this fertile valley,
but could not find it. When I asked about it, B4
explained that the new canal is covered, to reduce
evaporation in the desert heat, so you cannot see it
from the air. She added that the new canal carried
desalinated sea water, not water from the Colorado
River.
     About this time our airship turned north and we
were soon flying over the Salton Sea. B4 pointed to
it and said, "That once salty lake has been converted
into a fresh-water lake. All the salty water in it
was desalted and replaced by fresh water. The Great
Salt Lake in Utah and most other such lakes have been
similarly treated."
     "What do you do with the vast quantities of
salts and minerals extracted from salt water?" I
asked.
     "Salt has become one of our most widely used raw
materials. We use it to produce many chemicals,

plastics, and building materials. And the minerals
taken from salt water have largely replaced most
minerals taken from mines in your day."

I observed an odd-looking building complex which
emitted several tall plumes of steam and asked B4
what they were. She said they were steam from a geothermal power plant, and reminded me that there were
very large seas or beds of super-heated brine and
rock below the ground of this valley.

"But is not the entire surface of the earth
underlain by molten rock?" I enquired.

"Yes, that is true, but the depth of such rock
is less here than elsewhere, so it costs less to
reach and use geothermal sources here than elsewhere."

"What proportion of your total power is derived
from geothermal sources?" I asked.

"About one third. Solar power provides another
third, and all other sources, chiefly nuclear fusion
plants, the final third."

"Do you mean that you no longer use significant
quantities of natural gas, oil, and coal to produce
power?"

"Yes. We use our scarce and diminishing supplies of these raw materials in more productive ways,
chiefly to produce synthetic foods, fibres, and plastics. It seems incredible to us that they should
still have been used as fuel in your day. We especially regret your reckless consumption of irreplaceable deposits of petroleum and natural gas."

I noted with pleasure that all the land in the
valley around the old Salton Sea was now cultivated.
As we moved by Palm Springs, now rebuilt as a garden
city, I looked in vain for barren desert areas.

Soon we crossed a low mountain range and flew
over the old Mojave Desert, once an immense and
barren waste. It was entirely covered by cultivated
fields, immense greenhouses, and a few farm villages.
Every village had a lake beside it.

"Where does the water to irrigate this once
desert area come from?" I enquired.

"Nearly all of it comes from the Canadian North-
west by way of a chain of very large intermountain
lakes and covered canals which start above the Columbia River and run south behind the Sierra Nevada
mountain range. This waterway carries enough water
to irrigate all arid plateaus between the Rocky
Mountains and the Sierra Nevada Mountains along the
coast. There is another equally long and large canal
system which transports water from Hudson Bay, which

has been made a freshwater lake, by way of the Great Lakes, to the immense semi-arid prairies just east of the Rocky Mountains. All the once semi-arid and arid interior areas of North America are now supplied with ample supplies of fresh water, mostly from Northern Canada. Klondike water now flows all the way to northern Mexico."

"I do not see how it can be economic to transport water over such distances and use it for irrigation," I objected. "What technological breakthrough made it economic?"

"There have been no outstanding individual breakthroughs, merely steady technological progress for several centuries. The real cost of building dams and canals has been cut by over 80%. Moreover, we have learned to use irrigation water far more efficiently. We now get three to four times the crop yield per acre-foot of water customary in the U.S. of your day."

"With such water supplies and crop yields you must produce enormous food surpluses," I remarked.

"Indeed we do. North American is still by far the world's largest exporter of farm products."

5. Air Transport Again

After reaching the Mojave Desert our dirigible had turned west, and near the western end of the valley we passed over an immense and busy airport. B4 explained that it was the long-distance airport for the entire region around Los Angeles.

"Do you mean that in that area everyone who wants to fly across the country or abroad must travel 20 to 40 miles to reach this desert airport?" I asked.

"Yes, but they can travel the entire distance by freeway, and there is a tunnel through the San Gabriel Mountains behind Pasadena."

"But why is it placed so far from the garden cities in the Los Angeles area?"

"There are several important reasons for choosing this inland desert location. First, it is virtually free of fog, clouds, and rain which often delayed landings on airports nearer the coast. Secondly, its use does not create noise or air pollution over or near residential areas. Thirdly, planes landing or taking off here do not disturb TV reception in urban areas. Finally, by concentrating all long-distance air traffic from a wide area on this

-148-

airfield we can fly much larger planes, which radically reduces both costs per passenger mile and air
congestion. Many planes using this airport carry
over 1000 passengers. These are the major advantages. In addition, there are many minor ones, including all the other advantages of large-scale operation."

Soon we crossed the high, forested plateau behind Pasadena and approached our home airport. As we
descended, I noted again that there seemed to be no
airplanes on the local field.

"Is all air traffic to and from local airports
handled by airships?" I asked.

"Yes, we have found that airships are much qui-
eter, and also much cheaper for short hauls. The
take-off of an airship consumes much less fuel than
the take-off of an airplane of equal carrying capacity, and is much less noisy. Moreover, airships can
land on far smaller fields and can land more safely
on fog-bound fields."

"But isn't an airship take-off difficult and
dangerous when the wind is blowing hard?" I asked.

"Yes, but the number of such windy days here is
much less than the number of foggy or cloudy days.
And we can use extra buses as substitutes for airships on very windy days. Even on windless days,
buses handle most traffic to the International Airports."

"In my time," I continued, "many well-to-do
individuals owned and flew small private planes for
sport and business, and some futurists predicted a
vast increase in the number and use of such planes.
Yet I have seen very few small planes on this trip.
Why was this prediction a bad one?"

"We have largely given up the manufacture and
use of such planes for the same reasons that we have
drastically reduced the use of private cars. They
require an excessive amount of scarce metal and fuel.
And every flight of a small plane over an urban area
disturbs thousands of residents with its noise, air
pollution, and radio-wave interference. Furthermore, private planes cause air congestion and serious
accidents. However, there are still many private
clubs which have airfields and keep small planes in
areas remote from all urban centers. You rarely see
their planes because they are not allowed to fly over
or near urban areas or commercial plane routes."

6. A Stop for Tea

It was five o'clock in the afternoon, too late for my daily Voca lesson, when we disembarked from the dirigible at its home field. So, instead of returning directly to our apartment building, we stopped for tea at a restaurant in the central greenbelt through which we had to pass. The restaurant was set back several hundred feet from the sunken freeway, so that we could scarcely hear the traffic. It was completely surrounded by forest, gardens, and a small orange orchard. We sat down at a table in a patio beside the restaurant and ordered tea and a kind of hot bread strange to me.

"In my day," I began, "some health authorities claimed that both tea and coffee are harmful because they contain caffein, a drug tht overstimulates the heart. Do your doctors still hold this view and, if so, why do you still permit their use?"

"Our physicians still believe that frequent or regular use of caffein is harmful," B4 replied. "Nearly all the tea and coffee we drink has been de-caffeinated. Caffein is used only as a stimulant, and only under medical supervision."

"How about other stimulants, depressants, and mood-altering drugs, like marijuana and cocaine?" I queried.

"The use of all such drugs is also prohibited, except under medical supervision. Our scientists have demonstrated that in drug use, as in other fields, action produces equal reaction, and therefore artificial stimulation, depression, or other mood alteration is followed by an equal and opposite reaction. Hence, there is rarely a net benefit. Rather, artificial changes in moods are usually slightly harmful merely because they alter normal nervous processes. Moreover, many drugs are addictive. Of course, when one is mentally or physicallly ill, a temporary mood alteration may be beneficial, but only doctors can determine when this is so."

"In my day," I commented, "it was customary to serve cake with tea or coffee, yet no one here seems to be eating cake."

"The consumption of nearly all sweets—cake, cookies, pies, candies, etc.—has fallen almost continuously since your era because our knowledge of the harmful effects of such indulgence has grown steadily and because average intelligence and self-control has increased similarly. We do not prohibit the consumption of mild sweets, but all children are taught the harmful effects of consuming them, and there is a 100% special sales tax on the sale of sugar. Moreover, the sale of candy has long been prohibited because of the effects of candy-eating on teeth."

"But such control of personal behavior seems a serious violation of natural rights," I protested.

"For us the term natural right is as senseless as the term angel or soul. We recognize and consider only artificial legal rights. We believe that you used the term natural right primarily to justify behavior for which no scientific justification was possible. All the scientific evidence proves that consumption of caffein and candy is nearly always harmful, both to the consumer and to society. Therefore, we ban such consumption, except when prescribed by a physician."

By this time we had finished our tea, and I began to admire the ripe oranges on the trees in the adjoining grove. B4 noticed my behavior.

"Would you like to pick a few oranges to take home with you?" she asked.

"Do you mean anyone can pick fruit in such orchards?"

"Yes, that is the purpose for which such orchards are planted," she answered. "They are not commercial groves, but have been planted throughout our urban greenbelts in order to give city dwellers the pleasure of picking their own ripe fruit in season. Of course, you are supposed to limit your picking to the amount of fruit you can personally consume in a day or two. But all hikers and cyclists are encouraged to pick fruit, eat it on the spot, and take some home."

After paying our bill with a universal credit card, we walked to the orange grove and I picked three large ripe oranges to take home.

We arrived home about 6:30 and I went to my apartment to rest and dine alone. After supper I watched a circus performance on TV before retiring early, and turning on my sleep-teaching machine.

CHAPTER XII

A VISIT TO THE NEW NATIONAL CAPITAL

The next morning I again arose and breakfasted
an hour early in order to be ready for another planned trip outside the city, this time to Roosevelt,
the new capital of the United States. B4 came by to
pick me up at about 8 A.M., and we immediately left
for the nearby local bus station in the outer greenbelt. A quiet electric bus carried us directly to
the international airport in Antelope Valley, where
we took a large jet plan for Roosevelt. The plane
seemed little different in appearance from those of
my time, but was, of course, very much larger. After
we had settled ourselves in our seats, I began to
question B4 again.

1. Roosevelt, the National Capital

"You told me yesterday that the capital of the
U.S. is now a city called Roosevelt located in Eastern Colorado. Why was the capital moved from the
District of Columbia, and why is it named Roosevelt?"
"The capital was moved for two major reasons.
First, the center of North American population had
long been moving west and south, and is now within
200 miles of the new capital. Secondly, the climate
of Washington, D.C. was bad—hot and humid in the
summer, and cold and windy in the winter. The new
capital city has a near-perfect spring, summer, and
fall climate and a cold but invigorating winter
climate.
"As for the name, Roosevelt, we believe that his
administration introduced a new era in the U.S. and
world history. Moreover, he was the only American
president to win re-election three successive times."
"Just where in Colorado is the new capital
located?" I asked.
"It is near an old city once called Colorado
Springs, a famous resort city in your time," she said.
"What is the population of Roosevelt?" I asked.
"It is about the same as that of Los Angeles."
"But in my day," I objected, "the Washington
metropolitan area already had a population of over
two million, and was growing steadily. How could a
city of only half a million perform all the important
administrative, legislative, and judicial functions
once performed by a city four times as large,

especially since you have described a great increase
in these functions?"

"The answer in one word is decentralization.
Only the Congress and the senior executives and con-
sultants of each department of government work in the
national capital."

"But I thought that all government functions
once performed by local and state governments are now
performed or supervised by national agencies," I
countered. "Surely such a centralization of control
is the opposite of decentralization."

"It is true that all former functions of local
and state governments are now performed by national
agencies whose top officials work in Roosevelt," B4
said. "But centralization of function does not
require centralization of personnel and operations.
Our means of communication are so good and so cheap
that national and regional executives of national
agencies can supervise and control regional and local
officials without being present in person. In fact,
national executives of all national departments and
trusts make far fewer field trips now than they did
in your day. They no longer have to visit local
offices primarily to persuade state and local officials to cooperate with the national government.
They can now order them to do so by teletype, of
course, only after soliciting and studying local
objections."

2. Air Transport Speed

"How long will it take to reach Roosevelt?" I
asked.

"About one hour."

"But our best planes could make better time than
that," I remarked. "The distance is less than 1000
miles, and we had passenger planes that could fly
1500 miles an hour."

"We could build planes that would fly at over
3000 miles an hour," B4 replied. "Most of our passenger planes fly at less than 600 miles per hour in
order to save fuel and reduce accident rates. For
the past 400 years nearly all of our research efforts
in aviation have been directed at cost and accident
reduction, not at the achievement of higher speeds.
Your own rich oil reserves would have lasted much
longer if you had properly limited the speed of your
cars and planes."

"But six to ten hours in an airplane is very
tiring, and time is money," I objected.

"We have a few 1200 mile an hour planes flying
very long routes, like that from Los Angeles to Cal-
cutta, but they are expensive, and most tourists prefer to save money by taking slow sleeper planes.
Such planes are now so quiet and comfortable that it
is easy to get a good night's sleep on one of them."

Within ten minutes we were passing over the
Colorado River, which seemed perfectly dry. I looked
for the great lake behind Boulder Dam, but could not
find it.

"Where is Lake Mead?" I asked.

"It was over there, to the left, but of course
the entire lake was filled with sand and gravel
deposited by the river long ago. However, many new
dams have been built higher up.

3. Gambling and Inheritance

"Where is Las Vegas?" I asked. "In my day it
was fast becoming a large city."

"The growth of Las Vegas was due almost entirely
to regional differences in your gambling, liquor, and
prostitution laws. Las Vegas had, and still has, a
very bad climate. As soon as criminal laws became
uniform nationally, it began to decline in population
and is now only a small farm village."

"Do you still allow gambling?" I enquired.

"We have abolished all commercial gambling, and
all private gambling for high stakes. No one is
allowed to pay gambling debts by check, or to deposit
gambling gains in banks. But we permit people to
play bingo and other games for small coin stakes.
Such gambling yields much entertainment at a very
small cost."

"Have you abandoned lotteries also?"

"Yes, we abandoned both lotteries and high-stake
gambling centuries ago because we know that unearned
income is harmful to nearly all recipients. It
enables a few fortunate winners to live well without
working, and it makes family incomes more unequal.
The closer personal income is related to personal
production and thrift, the stronger is the economic
stimulus to optimum personal production and thrift."

"But," I protested, "your reasoning implies that
all inherited income is harmful. Have you also
abandoned inheritance?"

"Of course. We allow mates and children to
inherit cherished personal possessions, within
strict limits, but no one can inherit a significant
source of income. We believe that all personal money

-154-

income should consist of wages and interest on one's
own savings and earned pensions."

4. Forestry

We were soon passing over the Grand Canyon,
which was as impressive as ever. The adjacent forests seemed greener and denser than in my day.
"We feared the eventual destruction of our
forests by overcutting and air pollution," I said.
"Yet these forests seem in excellent condition. How
did you manage to preserve and improve them?"
"I have explained how we ended air pollution.
We also solved the problem of asexual reproduction
of most forest trees long ago, and this made steady
eugenic improvement of trees cheaper and faster than
ever. Our commercial forest trees have been improved as much as our people by eugenic selection.
The average forest acre now yields over five times as
much good lumber per acre as it did in your time. If
you look carefully, you will see an occasional small
plane crop dusting or spreading chemical fertilizer
on these forests. They are cared for as carefully
and efficiently as field crops."
"How do you minimize forest fires?" I asked.
"They consumed millions of acres of our forests every
year."
"We harvest or burn the underbrush each year
before the danger of forest fire is serious. We
learned long ago that controlled burning is the best
way to prevent uncontrolled burning. But we also use
hundreds of millions of tons of harvested brush and
undergrowth to manufacture paper, plastics, and
alcohol."
"Where are your largest remaining forests?" I
enquired.
"Our largest natural forests are in Canada and
Alaska, but our most productive commercial forests
are now located east of the Mississippi, where millions of the least fertile acres devoted to field
crops in your day have been returned to forest in
order to reduce soil erosion, increase pure water
supplies, improve the climate and provide more lumber
and wood pulp. As I have explained, the population
of this area has been very sharply reduced by
migration to the south, southwest, and west."

5. Racial Minorities

"This southwest region used to have many Indian

-155-

reservations," I remarked. "There were over 100,000 Navajo's living on one large reservation and trying to preserve their native culture. What has happened to them?"

"Nearly all of them left the reservation during the 21st century. All American Indians were fully assimilated long ago. The well-meaning efforts of some of your contemporaries to help the Indians preserve their culture were mistaken. They merely prolonged by a few decades the inevitable process of assimilation."

"Did the same thing happen to the large Mexican minorities in New Mexico and Texas?" I asked.

"Yes, but it took much longer. Over 30 million more Mexicans crossed the border during the century after you were frozen. This massive immigration, often illegal, was long tolerated by the American ruling class because it provided ample supplies of cheap labor and because it permitted millions of native Americans to shift from less desirable to more desirable jobs. But eventually it provoked English-speaking Americans to limit Mexican immigration strictly and effectively until the large Mexican-American population had been assimilated."

"But didn't you tell me once that the new North American Government now includes all of Mexico?" I asked.

"Yes, but the merger of Mexico into the North American state came much later."

"In my time," I commented, "the Mexicans were very proud of their distinctive Mexican culture and feared domination by 'gringos.' How did you induce them to consent to merge with the U.S. and Canada?"

"As Mexico experienced industrialization and modernization, it became more and more like the U.S. and other advanced countries, which gradually reduced opposition to American culture. But, since economic progres continued in the U.S., a very wide difference in real wages continued. Mexico eventually accepted the merger proposal primarily because it expected that a merger would rapidly raise Mexican real wages. And in fact the merger did double Mexican real wages within less than 20 years. Complete assimilation was eventually aided by the introduction of a new scientific language, Voca, throughout North America and all other countries."

6. The Appearance of Roosevelt

As we passed over the snow-covered Rocky

Mountains, I was again delighted by their majestic grandeur. Here, at least, there had been no observable change, no leveling and terracing of hills and mountains as along the Pacific Coast.

As soon as we had crossed the mountains we began to descend rapidly, and I caught my first glimpse of Roosevelt, the new national capital. To my surprise, it looked much like the new Los Angeles, except that the trees were of different varieties. There was a distinct city center surrounded by a wide greenbelt, and beyond the greenbelt there was a ring of satellite towns, each surrounded by its own greenbelt through which a single freeway ran.

"Is every city in North America a replica of the new Los Angeles?" I asked.

"In major respects, yes," B4 replied. "All are near the optimum size, all are laid out so as to minimize street traffic, especially the use of private cars, all are decentralized, and all are planned so as to facilitate stable community life. We have found that the universal application of these planning principles makes all cities much alike. However, if my memory serves me well, your own contemporaries constantly complained about the uniform appearance of cities throughout America."

"Yes, I did so myself," I said, "but I was really complaining about uniform ugliness, not uniformity itself."

Our plane landed gently on a large international airport about five miles outside Roosevelt, and we immediately transferred to an electric bus parked beside our plane and rode in it over greenbelt freeways to a very large and tall hotel on the margin of the city center. At the hotel we rented a small electric car and set out immediately to explore the city.

7.   The National Legislature

"What would you like to see first?" B4 asked.

"I would like to visit the new Capitol Building, or its equivalent, and listen in on a session of your Congress."

"Very well," B4 said, "we shall proceed there immediately. I know it is in session because I checked in advance, and I also arranged for our admission to the gallery."

As we proceeded towards the new Capitol, she explained that the national legislature now consisted of only one house of just one hundred members.

"Why did you abandon the two-house legislature?"
I asked.

"We found that the requirement that every law be
approved by two entirely separate legislative bodies
involved great duplication of effort and much delay.
As the scope and scale of legislation increased, the
work of the Congress became so heavy that it could
not be handled by a two-body legislature. Therefore,
the Senate was abolished late in the 21st century.

The Capitol was less than half a mile from the
hotel, so it did not take long to reach it. I had
expected to find a great domed building and was surprised when we stopped at a large office building.
It was a very handsome building but it had no special
park around it and no dome on top of it. As we
entered, B4 explained that the legislative chamber
was on the 10th floor, in the center of the building,
and that the building contained offices for all
members of Congress and their local staffs.

"It must be much easier for members to answer
quorum calls now that they have offices in the building where the legislative chamber is located," I
remarked.

"Yes, but quorum calls can be answered and votes
on proposed laws registered by each legislator in his
office. He merely inserts a unique key in an electronic device and pushes one of several buttons to
register his presence or his vote."

"But doesn't this make it too easy for legislators to ignore debates in the legislative chamber?"
I objected. "We believed that such debates were and
should be very influential in determining legislative
decisions."

"That belief was already largely obsolete in
your day, and long ago became entirely false," B4
continued. "Debates in the legislature were and are
largely intended to influence public opinion. Legislators usually make up their minds before legislative
debates occur, and, if they later change them, they
often do so because of something they have read, not
something they have heard in a legislative debate.
Today, all formal debates between legislators are
held in special TV studios and are broadcast throughout the country. When legislators are assembled in
the national legislature, which occurs only once a
week, they spend their time asking questions of committee chairmen, not debating with each other.
Today, as in your time, nearly all serious study and
discussion of proposed legislation occurs in

committees."

By now we had entered and seated ourselves in
the gallery, which ran entirely around the legislature chamber. I noted that the chamber had only
about forty seats, each with a handsome desk in
front of it.

"If the Congress has 100 members, why are there
only 40 seats on the floor?" I asked.

"Because there are rarely more than 20 members
on the floor at one time. This was usually true even
in your time, when members had to appear on the floor
to vote and answer quorum calls."

In fact, at the moment, I could count only seven
persons occupying legislative seats.

"But where do they sit when the President or
some foreign dignitary addresses the Congress?" I
asked.

"Such speeches are delivered only on TV, and
members listen to them in their offices, if they wish
to hear them."

At this point the Chairman of the Committee on
Foreign Affairs arose from his chair and began to
address the national legislature. We picked up the
earphone attached to our seat and began to listen.
I now knew enough Voca to understand most, if not
all, of his speech. He was discussing the foreign
aid program for the next five years, which provided
for an annual appropriation equal to about 4% of
North American GNP. He explained that average North
American real income was still over twice as high as
such income in Africa and Asia, and argued that the
proposed income redistribution would create good will
towards North America and would increase economic
welfare in poorer countries much more than it would
decrease it in North America. Moreover, he claimed,
most North Americans were benevolent by education and
heredity and would therefore gain substantial satisfaction from knowledge of the continuance of their
altruistic foreign aid program. I was surprised to
note that he made no reference to ethical or moral
obligation.

"Who is the speaker," I asked in a whisper.

"He is Legislator 8S," B4 replied. "He comes
from the region you called Texas, but of course he
does not represent the people of his region or any
other. The national legislature consists entirely of
social scientists chosen by social scientists. 8S was
trained primarily as a political economist, and was
elected by a specialized section of the North American Economic Association, the national association of

-159-

his profession."

When the first speaker had completed his brief speech, a second speaker arose and began to use similar arguments to justify a foreign aid program amounting to 5% of North American GNP. In the course of his speech he made clear to me that all such aid was administered by a department of the World Federal Union, not by any individual nation.

When he finished, a third speaker arose and proposed that the question should be submitted to a national vote. He argued that this was an issue on which laymen had strong feelings, and one which they could understand as well as any social scientist. Only individiual voters, he claimed, could sense directly the degree of their own benevolence. And voters would gain more personal satisfaction from altruistic acts which they had personally and actively approved. Therefore, all citizens should be allowed and encouraged to vote on this issue. In conclusion, he moved the adoption of his proposal, which was immediately seconded. The voting was done electronically, without requiring legislators to appear in person, and the results were displayed on a large electronic wall panel. It soon became apparent that the motion had carried by a large majority.

"It seems to me," I remarked, "that the persuasive arguments for a popular vote we have just heard are really arguments for democratic government and against what you call government by experts."

"Our theory of government by experts does not require that all social problems be solved by experts," B4 said. "We allow the voters to decide all issues on which they are well informed and/or in which they are emotionally involved. For instance, they must approve major new laws on sex, aborton, eugenics, the volume of saving, etc. But they are not asked to vote on laws controlling foreign trade, wage rates, price determination, methods of taxation, banking, investment, and innumerable other complex issues which social scientists are much more competent to deal with, and in which most voters have little if any interest."

"But surely voters are very much interested in how much taxes they pay," I objected.

"Indeed they are, and they can vote to increase or reduce total spending on any major government function. For instance, they vote every five years on whether to spend a larger or smaller share of GNP on education. They are told in advance precisely which educational services will probably be expanded

or contracted as a result of their vote. But voters
cannot vote on the methods of education because
educational techniques should be determined by
experts."

I had noticed that all the legislators in the
chamber appeared young as well as healthy and handsome. Some looked like they had just graduated from
college.

"Do you allow persons in their twenties to serve
as national lawmakers?" I asked.

"No, all must be over 30, and the average age is
about 45. They look young to you because eugenic
measures have made all adults look younger for their
age than in your time."

"We had many aged persons in our Congress," I
resumed. "Indeed, our Congress was dominated by aged
persons, because of the seniority rule, but I see no
aged persons here. Do you give less weight to
seniority?"

"Yes, the seniority rule was abolished long ago.
The chairperson of each legislative committee is
selected entirely on the basis of his ability. Moreover, we have an upper as well as a lower age limit
for national legislators. No one over 70 is allowed
to serve."

"But doesn't wisdom increase with age?"

"Some kinds of wisdom in some men continue to
grow after age 70. But physical stamina and I.Q.
begin to decline long before age 70. And the job of
serving as a national legislator is very demanding.
We permit legislators to serve to age 70 only because
our 70-year-olds are more vigorous and mentally alert
than were your 50-year olds."

"Are lobbyists as numerous, active, and influential in Roosevelt as they were in Washington, D.C. in
1980?" I queried.

"We have no professional lobbyists. Our legislators and senior executives are all highly educated
experts familiar with the literature of their specialty. They could learn little from lobbyists, and
would be very suspicious of their motives and advice.
Moreover, even if lobbyists were learned and honest,
they should not be allowed to use their expertise to
influence public policy for personal, sectarian,
regional, group, or political benefit. When our
legislators want expert advice or information, they
rely solely on government employees, research scientists, and university professors, not on biased
lobbyists."

"But in my day," I protested, "lobbyists were often able to supply useful information and advice."

"Yes, so I have read, but that was because you had government by half-educated or uneducated politicians. We have government by experts who need no information from lobbyists."

8. The Chief Executive

By this time the noon hour had arrived and the legislature adjourned for lunch. We left the gallery and went to a quick-lunch center, where we bought sandwiches and drinks to consume in our electric cart. We did not want to waste the time required to eat a regular lunch in a restaurant during the noon-time rush. Instead, we returned to our cart and began to explore the city as we lunched. We went first to visit the residence of the President of North America, which was only a few blocks from the building occupied by the National Legislature. The residence seemed quite small and unpretentious. Only the guard posts and fence distinguished it from nearby houses.

"Our White House was far larger and more impressive than this residence," I commented.

"Indeed it was, or rather is," B4 said. "It is still preserved in good condition as a major historical relic and tourist attraction in Washington, D.C. The center of that city, including all the important buildings, is now preserved for much the same reasons that you restored and preserved Williamsburg, the old colonial capital of Virginia."

"But why is the new home of the president so much smaller than the old?"

"For two major reasons. First, your White House was more an administrative office than a home. We have almost entirely separated the two. You may recall that the British had always done this. Their prime ministers lived in an unimpressive residence, 10 Downing Street, when the British Empire extended throughout the world. Secondly, the salary of our President is only twice that of the average worker and he cannot afford to hire personal servants. He does all his official entertaining in a state banquet hall at state expense."

"How is your President chosen?" I asked.

"He is chosen by the National Legislature from among the heads of the twenty major national trusts and departments, who correspond to your cabinet."

"Do you mean that no legislator can become President? And if not, why not?"

"Our President has only administrative functions. He has been professionally educated in public and business administration and has had at least 20 years of administrative experience. He has done little graduate work in social science and has had no legislative experience. He has no legislative functions, except to recommend changes in methods of administration. He cannot veto any laws, or recommend laws on non-administrative matters. We entrust administration and legislation only to experts in these fields. Experts in legislation are not qualified by education or experience to serve as presidents."

"But if legislators are not competent to serve as administrators, how can they select the top administrator wisely?" I objected.

"You have a good point there," B4 said. "But, since their choice is restricted to the experienced and proven top executives of major government agencies, they cannot go far wrong. And we think it wise that the President should be subordinate to the National Legislature. Therefore, he is not only chosen by them, but is also removable by them at any time. This assures that he will enforce the laws and policies they approve."

9. Insurance and Investment

From the presidential mansion we drove to the center of a nearby satellite town, a center which contained only two large tall buildings. B4 explained that one of them housed the national office of the Insurance Department, and the other the national office of the Investment Trust. She added that they were the only export plants in this town, and that together they employed about 20,000 workers, nearly all of whom lived in the surrounding town, within one mile of their place of employment.

"Why do you call one a trust and the other a department?" I asked.

"Trusts provide goods sold for a price; Departments produce free goods, like health care and insurance."

"In my day," I objected, "most insurance was sold for a price. Are all insurance services now free goods?"

"Indeed they are," B4 answered. "We believe that all persons should be insured against all risks,

-163-

and the easiest way to assure such coverage is to
make all insurance a free good. Moreover, by making
insurance a free good we have eliminated all insurance selling costs. We have also made it unnecessary
to issue individual insurance policies and collect
millions of premiums. This has cut insurance costs
per dollar of benefit payment by over 50%."

"But doesn't universal coverage of all risks
greatly increase insurance costs?" I objected.

"It increases benefit payments, but not national
real costs," she said. "An insurance system redis-
tributes income and property losses, it does not
cause them. In fact, it reduces many kinds of losses
by allocating them to those partly or entirely
responsible for them."

"How do you allocate the costs of compulsory
insurance to those responsible for insured losses?"
I enquired.

"We allocate the costs of most auto accidents to
those responsible for them by imposing special insur-
ance-financing taxes on gasoline and tires. As a
result, those car users who drive the most miles at
the fastest speeds, and therefore cause the most
accidents, pay the highest auto-insurance premiums.
Moreover, fire insurance is largely financed by taxes
on flammable building materials and furnishings which
vary with the fire risk their use creates. And theft
insurance is largely financed by sales taxes on the
most frequently stolen consumers' goods."

"I conclude," I remarked, "that every citizen
has full insurance against all risks without having
to make any personal effort or decision to secure it.
That must go far to simplify life and reduce worry in
your society. I was always worried about my expensive and incomplete insurance protection."

"What does the Investment Trust do?" I asked.

"The Investment Trust assembles all investment
funds collected by the National Credit Bank as voluntary private savings and adds to them the savings
created by the national government through taxation,
i.e., by forced social saving. It allocates these
savings to the head offices of other national departments and Trusts. It does not try to evaluate the
economic or social desirability of individual local
investment proposals because it knows that each
national agency is better qualified to evaluate such
projects in its industry."

"How does the Investment Trust decide how much
to allocate to each national agency?" I enquired.

"Each agency gives the Investment Trust a loan

=164=

demand schedule showing how much it will borrow at
each possible rate of interest. The Trust then fixes
a uniform national rate of interest which will equal-
ize or balance total supply and demand for loan
funds."

"What happens when a borrower makes unsound
local investments?"

"Usually profits on some local investments offset losses on others. Of course, if any agency makes
too many or too large bad investments, the head of
the agency is demoted and replaced by a more capable
manager. However, we never close plants and discharge workers after bad investments. Instead, we
normally operate at a loss until growing demand has
made a bad investment profitable. In those rare
cases when demand does not grow, we remodel the old
plant and start producing new products, but continue
to pay reduced wages to any temporarily idle workers.
No workers ever have to relocate due to bad investments. Since each agency is a monopoly, demand is
relatively easy to predict, and gross overinvestment
is rare."

10. A Megastructure Village

From the town center we drove next to a village
of some 6,000 population in the same town. It consisted of ten big four-story garden apartment buildings grouped around a large park containing a nursery
school, a clinic, a supermarket, and other village-
center facilities. B4 explained that all of the
buildings were linked by underground pedestrian
tunnels which were heated in the winter.

"Why do you have such villages here and not in
Southern California?" I asked.

"Because the climate is much colder here in
winter. The colder the winter climate, the larger
the number of people who prefer to live in such villages and communities. In Canada and Siberia many
satellite towns consist entirely of such villages,
which are linked to town centers by underground
tunnels, so that in cold weather the inhabitants
spend little if any time outdoors, except for winter
sports."

11. The Treasury Department and Taxation

After driving around the megastructure village,
we traveled through other villages and across the
intervening greenbelt to the town center of another

-165-

town. B4 pointed out two of the largest buildings
and explained that they housed the national offices
of the Treasury Department and the Health Department.
I noticed again that there were no parking lots for
private cars, and that the street traffic consisted
almost entirely of pedestrians and cyclists. I also
noted that the building occupied by the Treasury
Department was much smaller than that of the Health
Department.

"In my day," I commented, "our Treasury Department had many more employees than our national health
agency, yet here the opposite seems to be true."

"The collection of taxes is now far simpler than
in your time," B4 said. "We have only a score of
national trusts, and they pay their taxes directly to
the national treasury. All taxes on individuals are
collected by the National Credit Bank, which deducts
them from personal bank accounts and remits them to
the national office of the Banking Trust, which
merely transfers the total taxes monthly to the
Treasury Department. As a result, the Treasury
Department is able to collect all national taxes at a
minimum cost.

"On the other hand, the Health Department super-
vises all regional and local health services which
together employ over 15% of the total population."

"What are your chief forms of taxation?"

"Over 80% of our national revenue is derived
from a universal poll tax which amounts on the average to about half of personal income."

"We considered poll taxes to be very regressive,"
I countered. "Why do you prefer them to progressive
income taxes?"

"Unlike poll taxes, income taxes fall on marginal income and are therefore a serious deterrant to
work and thrift. Moreover, our personal incomes are
ideally determined, and therefore require no correc-
tion by progressive income taxes."

"Do the lowest-paid workers pay the same poll
tax as the highest-paid workers?"

"Yes, and we consider this desirable for several
reasons. If poll taxes varied with income, they
would reduce the rewards for marginal output. Moreover, nearly all the costs of government are social
overhead costs which, like business fixed costs, do
not rise when a worker increases his personal output
and income. Finally, although poll taxes are regressive, the distribution of free goods or benefits
received by individuals from government is equally
regressive."

At this point, B4 glanced at her watch and said
we had better return to the car rental office, turn
in our car and board a bus for the airport if we were
to catch our 4 o'clock plane back to Los Angeles.
This process was uneventful. When we were finally in
the sky on our way home, I began to question B4
again.

12. On Boredom in Utopia

"In my day," I observed, "critics of utopian
novels often argued that life in a utopia would be
dull and pointless because there would be no personal
or social problems to solve. They asserted that men
needed at least occasional danger and tragedy, to
make life interesting."
"Yes, I have read of that argument," B4 said.
"But many of those who stated it believed in a utopian after-life, a heaven where there would be no evil
and no problems to solve. Few if any men ever rejected the idea of heaven on the ground that it would
be free from problems and sufferings."
"You have detected an obvious but generally
ignored inconsistency," I replied, "but you have not
really answered their argument."
"Quite right! I will now try to do so. First,
I reject the idea that most utopian writers thought
of or described utopia as a society without personal
pain and social problems. I believe that most of them
were merely trying to describe a society in which the
most serious and most easily solvable personal and
social problems had been largely solved and in which
men were using sound scientific methods to solve
remaining problems. Secondly, I contend that the
number of such remaining problems is always infinite.
For instance, the mere fact that men are instinct-
ively curous means that men will always want to
increase their knowledge, which assures an infinite
supply of intellectual problems. Likewise, the fact
that human economic wants are innumerable and, in
total, insatiable, implies that no amount of economic
progress can eliminate the basic economic problem of
maximizing economic production with a limited supply
of land, labor, and capital goods."
For the rest of the air trip home I was absorbed
by the grand scenery under us. We arrived at the Los
Angeles International Airport about 6 P.M. and got
home by 6:30.
Before she left me, B4 explained that she could
not see me tomorrow, but that Professor OB would call

-167-

for me at 7 A.M. in the morning to take me on another trip, this time to the capital of the new world government, Honolulu.

After she left, I had supper alone, watched a Chinese dance program on TV, and went to bed early.

CHAPTER XIII

THE WORLD CAPITAL

The next morning OB knocked on my apartment door
quite early because we planned to have breakfast on
the plane to Honolulu. We traveled by electric cart
to the border of the town, where we took an express
bus to the international airport. It was a beautiful
spring day. Many trees and bushes were in flower. I
realized more fully than ever before how attractive a
garden city free of private cars and smog could be.

On the trip to the airport, OB informed me that
we would travel on a supersonic plane which would
cover the distance between Los Angeles and Honolulu
in about 90 minutes so that we would be able to do
several hours of sightseeing in Honolulu and return
to Los Angeles by bedtime.

1. International Transport

We arrived at the international airport about
8 A.M. and were carried to the plane in a giant airport bus, but it seemed narrow and endless after we
had entered it.

"How long is this plane, and how many passengers
does it carry?" I enquired.

"It is about 400 feet long and it can carry over
1,000 passengers,"

When I looked incredulous, he added that the
plane had three decks, and that we were on the second
deck.

I wondered how long it would take to fill such a
large plane, but was agreeably surprised to see it
fill up very quickly. When I looked around I observed that passengers were entering our deck from eight
different doors, four on each side of the plane, and
that each door served a separate seating section.
Before the plane moved, every seat was taken.

"Our planes used to fly less than half full most
of the time," I commented, "yet this plane is completely full. How do you manage to achieve such an
occupancy rate?"

"There are two main methods," OB replied.
"First, our air transport industry is organized as a
monopoly, which makes it much easier to predict the
volume of traffic. Secondly, we auction off all
unsold seats shortly before each long-distance plane
departs."

"Do you mean that there are always people waiting in every airport ready to bid on unsold seats?" I asked. "I should think not many persons would want to start on a long trip without a reserved seat, especially in a society as prosperous as yours"

"We have many young people eager to see the world at minimum cost. And some retired people also like to save money. When demand for seats is relatively low, auction prices fall very low, which attracts more travelers. The average price for auctioned seats is about 60% of full fares, but they may fall much lower on occasion."

"But surely it is most inconvenient to have to pack and come to the airport without knowing for sure whether a plane seat is available," I remonstrated.

"Yes, it was," OB conceded, "but we abandoned that system long ago. Today all auctions for unfilled seats are conducted by radio, two or more hours before the plane leaves. Bidders make bids by telephone from their homes, and are quickly notified as to their success. They never leave their homes until they know they have a reserved seat."

OB had reserved a window seat for me, and I made full use of it as we departed. Before the plane had risen too high, I noticed some very odd looking ships in the ocean. They seemed to have rows of square metallic sails.

"Have you revived the use of sailing ships?" I asked.

"Yes, due to the increased real cost of fuel and to improved technology in sailing, we have found it economic to move a large volume of ocean freight by sailing ships."

"What have been the major advances in sailing-ship technology," I asked.

"All modern sailing ships are made of steel and use aluminum sails, which resemble your Venetian blinds. The sails need not be furled or unfurled. They remain in the same attitude at all times. Only the inclination of the metal strips needs to be altered to catch more or less wind, and this is done by machinery not by human power."

"Can they tack against the wind?" I queried.

"Yes, but they are used chiefly on routes which require little tacking."

'Isn't it difficult for such large ships to enter and move about in modern harbors and docks?" I protested.

"All of them have small emergency motors for use in calms, storms, and harbors. And sailing ships rely even more on tugs than do motor ships."

"In my time," I remarked, "tankers carried more
than half of all tonnage moved by ocean freighters,
yet I have yet to see a tanker."

"Yes, that is a great change," OB said. "Today
we rarely use petroleum or its products as a fuel.
Nearly all petroleum is used as a raw material to
produce rubber, plastics, and chemicals in processing plants located near the oil fields. Of course,
the annual world production of petroleum is over 90%
smaller today than in your era."

2. WFU Armed Forces and Police

"I have also seen no warships," I observed.

"All warships are owned and operated by the
World Federal Union," OB explained, "and the home
port for most of them is Honolulu. Moreover, the WFU
navy is much smaller than the U.S. navy in your day.
It consists largely of nuclear-powered aircraft carriers."

"Are the other armed forces of the WFU equally
small?" I asked.

"Yes, the total military force of the WFU
amounts to less than 500,000 persons. The air force
is the largest branch of the armed force because the
WFU relies heavily upon surveillance from the air to
detect military threats, and upon bombing raids to
repress rebellion. The WFU land forces are very
small."

"Is the WFU air force armed with nuclear weapons?"

"Yes, but they have not been used for over a
century. We now have large numbers of nonexplosive
bombs which release gases that temporarily disable
all persons who breathe them. The use of such gases
has enabled the WFU to suppress all recent military
resistance with few if any deaths and with little
property damage. Of course, if any rebels or terrorists learned how to protect themselves against WFU
gas bombs, the WFU would resort to more destructive
weapons, perhaps even neutron bombs, but this is most
unlikely."

"How do you minimize political terrorism and
armed rebellion?"

"The production of all nuclear and other decis-
ive military weapons is concentrated in a very small
number of closely guarded plants, located on Pacific
islands firmly controlled by the WFU, and there is

-171-

no commercial trade in such weapons. All are owned
and used by the armed forces of the WFU.

"Moreover, no private person or group is able to
accumulate and spend enough money to bribe employees
of munitions plants or military offices in order to
secure weapons. As I explained previously, all substantial payments must be made by check, and all
personal bank statements are reviewed by the police.

"Finally, the WFU has its own international
police and spy network which constantly seeks to
uncover secret terrorist and subversive organizations and activities."

"What would the WFU do if a civil war broke out
within a member state?"

"That would depend largely upon the circumstan-
ces," OB explained. "If the legitimate national
government seemed able to repress the rebellion without using illegal weapons, the WFU might do nothing.
If the rebels used any nuclear or other illegal
weapons, or if they made use of foreign troops or aid,
the WFU would immediately intervene on the side of
the established government. On the other hand, if
the established government appeared unable to quickly
suppress a rebellion, the WFU would require both
sides to cease fighting and accept the results of a
democratic election supervised by the World Federal
Union."

3. The Location of the World Capital

At this point our conversation was interrupted
by a stewardess who brought us our breakfast. The
plane was now so high and we were so far from land
that I did not mind taking my eyes off the scene
below.

After a delicious breakfast of food which still
seemed strange and exotic to me, I began to question
OB again.

"Why was Honolulu chosen as the capital of the
World Federal Union?" I asked.

"The first effective world government was established jointly by the U.S. and the U.S.S.R. late in
the 21st century, and Honolulu is on an island between these two great superpowers. It remained the
capital after all other countries were admitted as
voting members of the WFU because it is conveniently
placed between populous Asia and the two Americas.
Moreover, being a multi-racial city located on an
isolated island no longer a part of the United
States, it is relatively free from national

domination or undue influence exerted by one nation
or race. Even in your time, Honolulu was a success-
ful integrated multi-racial community. It is even
more multi-racial today."
    'In my century," I commented, "Europe was still
the economic, cultural, and political center of the
world. For us, it would have seemed far more sensible to locate the capital of a new world government
in Switzerland or Austria rather than in then
remote Honolulu. Why has the prestige of Europe
declined?"
    "It is not so much that Europe has declined as
that Asia and the two Americas have developed much
faster. Today, Australia and New Zealand have a
combined European population larger than that of
France and England combined, partly because the popu-
lations of all countries on the continent of Europe
have declined sharply. And the population of the two
Americas is over twice as large as the populatin of
Europe. The population of Asia has of course declined much more than the population of Europe, but it is
still very large."
    "What was the reason for this great population
change?" I asked.
    "It was almost entirely a natural adjustment of
population size to local resources, both natural and
cultural. Asia was culturally backward, as well as
grossly overpopulated, in your day, and most Asian
nations adopted radical population control measures
during the 21st century. European population declined less rapidly because Europe had a very advanced
culture, but exhaustion of its natural resources and
the ease of emigration to North America, South America, Australasia, and Siberia resulted in a gradual
but prolonged population decline after about 2050
A.D."

    4. WFU Structure and Functions

    "Is the World Federal Union democratic?" I en-
quired.
    "It is partly democratic and partly meritocrat-
ic. The World Parliament is a one-chamber representative body in which simple basic decisions of wide
general interest are made democratically, but it has
delegated nearly all complex or detailed legislative
decisions to experts chosen by experts."
    "What proportion of all legislative decisions
have been delegated to experts?" I asked.
    "Over 90%, OB replied. "The World Parliament

reserves for itself only those problems which laymen can understand and which deeply interest most voters. For instance, the Parliament decided to create a new world language only after a two-thirds majority support among world citizens for this policy had developed. But it assigned the task of creating a new world language to a staff of experts headed by an expert chosen by the appropriate world professional associations."

"I am still not clear as to the nature of this division of functions. Could you give me another example and explanation?" I said.

"Yes, of course," he replied. "Most voters and lay legislators are deeply interested in problems of world peace and are competent to decide whether or not the WFU should use military force to preserve peace. Therefore, the armed forces of the WFU cannot independently initiate or end major military measures against a nation threatening world peace, but, once the World Parliament has approved such measures, the experts who manage the WFU armed forces make all decisions concerning how these measures are carried out. They also make all decisions concerning the peace-time training and equipment of such forces, and concerning the promotion of individual officers, except that individual nations must be represented in the armed forces in proportion to their representation in the World Parliament. Thus the officer corps is a self-ruling and self-perpetuating body of military experts."

"But isn't there a danger that senior military officers might decide to overthrow the legal WFU government and declare their leader a world dictator or emperor?" I objected.

"Yes, this danger has always existed in every nation ruled by civilians," OB conceded. "The only protection against it is proper indoctrination of potential military personnel before and after they become members of the armed forces. Most of the advanced nations of your own time had already mastered such indoctrination. No English-speaking nation ever experienced a military coup in your age. The danger of such a coup, after several hundred more years of civilian rule, is less than ever today. The traditional English attitude of your time has become the dominating world attitude towards civilian control over military forces."

"One of the chief obstacles to the creation of a democratic world government in my day," I remarked, "was the great variation in culture and real income

-174-

per person among the nations of the world. A democratic world government would have been overwhelm-
ingly dominated by the poorest and least educated
peoples. How have you avoided this evil?"

"First, the combined total population of the
most advanced nations has actually increased, partly
due to migration, while that of the least advanced
nations had declined sharply, which has greatly
reduced differences in culture and real income per
person. Secondly, the World Federal Union is still
not fully democratic. Representation in the Parliament of the WFU is based upon national GNP, not
upon national population. Thirdly, the WFU constitution allows each nation to control its own immigration policies, and also forbids all compulsory
redistribution of territory and wealth among nations."

"The constitution of the U.S. prohibited state
control over trade and migration, but permitted the
central government to redistribute wealth and income
among states and social classes. Why didn't the WFU
constitution contain similar provisions?" I inquired.

"Because this would have permitted enough poor
people to migrate from poor to rich nations to cause
a sharp fall in the standard of living in all advanced countries, and would also have created serious
assimilation problems. Moreover, it would have permitted a world government dominated by poor nations
to enrich those nations at the expense of rich
nations, or vice versa. The advanced nations refused
to submit themselves to rule by a world government
until they were assured of both continued control
over their own immigration policies and freedom from
compulsory international wealth-equalization policies."

"I assume that the chief function of the WFU is
to prevent war and preserve peace by settling all
international disputes peacefully," I remarked. "How
does it do this?"

"It requires that all international disputes be
submitted to the World Court established by the WFU
in Honolulu. This court interprets and applies an
extensive body of international law enacted by the
Parliament of the WFU."

"What are the other major functions of the WFU?"
I enquired.

"It has created a new international monetary
unit, the only one used in member nations, and it
regulates the quantity of it in such a way as to
prevent world inflation or deflation.

"It regulates all foreign trade, primarily in order to assure free trade between all nations.

"It regulates all sources of significant international air and water pollution.

"I controls all activities in outer space.

"It maintains both an open and a secret inspection service whose function is to detect research on, and/or the production of, illegal military weapons by member nations.

"It maintains military forces, largely naval and air, to be used to preserve international peace.

"It regulates oceanic fishing, whaling, sealing, etc., and the recovery of ocean-bottom mineral ores in international waters.

"It governs Antarctica.

"It regulates all international communication, but only to reduce the cost and improve the performance of such communication.

"It owns and operates all international transport and communication agencies.

"It owns and operates all major munitions plants."

"How is the WFU financed?" I asked.

"All governments today are largely financed by a uniform poll tax because poll taxes do not fall on marginal income and thereby reduce incentives to work and save. The WFU imposes a supplementary poll tax, now about 10% of each national poll tax, on all adults of member countries."

"Do you mean that adults in the poorest countries pay the same poll tax as those in the richest countries?" I enquired.

"No, because the national poll tax varies from nation to nation, being highest in the richest nations and lowest in the poorest nations. For instance, it is more than twice as high in North America as in India."

"But doesn't the WFU provide the same service to all adults?" I objected.

"Yes, but the allocation of WFU costs among nations is based upon ability to pay because this helps to assure political support for the WFU among poorer nations."

"Which nations are the poorest and the richest today?" I queried.

"In per person real income, large nations rank about the same as in your day. The main differences are that all small nations have been absorbed into larger nations, and that income differences both within and between large nations have been radically

reduced. For instance, average real income in India
is now almost half of the North American level,
whereas in your time it was less than one tenth of
this level."

5. The Fate of Israel

"In my time," I remarked, "the conflict between
Moslems and Jews over the future of Palestine was a
major threat to world peace because the Soviets supported the Arabs and the Americans supported the
Zionists. Moreover, Moslem wealth and population was
growing much faster than Israel's wealth and population. How was this conflict finally settled?"
"The conflict continued for several decades
after you were frozen, and twice threatened to cause
a Soviet-American war. To end the threat to world
peace, the U.S. and the U.S.S.R. eventually subsi-
dized the migration of most Israeli Jews to other
countries."
"Do you mean they were forced to leave the land
of their ancestors?"
"Very few were physically coerced. When the
U.S. ended its massive subsidies to Israel and offered equally large subsidies for Israeli migration to
other countries, the great majority of Israelis chose
voluntarily to leave Palestine. Later, discrimination against Jews by the succeeding Moslem Palestin-
ian Government caused continuing migration."
"Where did the Israeli Jews migrate to?" I
inquired.
"Over 80% of them migrated to English-speaking
countries, mostly to North America, where Jews had
been relatively prosperous and free from discrimination. To aid this migration, the U.S. and Canada
ended all visa requirements for Israeli Jews, and
also guaranteed housing and generous welfare aid for
five years."
"But didn't the abandonment of Israel create
lasting, world-wide Jewish dislike and hatred of
Americans?"
"It did arouse great temporary antagonism among
devoted Zionists, but the outstanding economic and
social success of the new Jewish immigrants in the
U.S. soon ended this antagonism."

6. Arrival at Honolulu—No Customs

By now our plane had begun its descent towards
the Honolulu International Airport, and I gazed with

admiration at the verdant green island, the beautiful beaches, and the radically transformed city of Honolulu. The luxury hotels crowded together along Waikiki Beach had been replaced by a line of more colorful and more coordinated 12-story hotels, each set in the midst of a tropical garden. And the congested, sky-scraper-studded central business district had been replaced by a new, planned, greenbelt-encircled city center much like that of the new Los Angeles. Here, too, auto traffic had been almost entirely replaced by pedestrians, cyclists, and slow electric buses.

When our plane had landed, I noticed that neither we nor our fellow passengers had to pass through customs. OB explained that all nations long ago had abolished tariffs and customs services, at the order of the WFU.

"But doesn't free trade enable poor countries to depress wage levels in rich countries like the U.S.?" I asked OB, as we rode into Honolulu on an electric bus.

"Of course not," he replied. "Even your better economists knew that free trade raises real wages in all countries. Your legislators voted for tariffs only because they wanted to secure campaign contributions and votes from special interests eager to benefit themselves at the expense of the average consumer, who made no large campaign contributions."

"Well," I remarked, "whether or not free trade benefits the consumer, it certainly benefits travelers. I always found going through customs to be both tedious and irritating. But if you have no customs officers, how do you prevent importation of illegal drugs?"

"Dealing in drugs is now both unprofitable and easy to detect because all large payments must be made by check and reported on bank statements reviewed by computers and police. Moreover, the social causes of drug addiction and crime have been largely eliminated."

7. Sightseeing

We got off the bus at the nearest satellite town center and rented an electric cart as a more convenient and leisurely means of sightseeing. We drove around the town center, and OB called my attention to the tallest and largest building, a handsome pink concrete structure with large mosaic murals on its outer walls.

"I presume that is an export firm, the chief employer in this town," I remarked. "What activity does it house?"

"It houses the headquarters staff of the WFU air force," OB informed me. "All the major departments of the WFU government are housed in such satellite town centers so that nearly all the employees can walk or cycle to work in less than fifteen minutes. The city center contains only the WFU headquarters and those offices and facilities used by residents in all satellite towns."

After inspecting the town center, we set out for the city center. On the way I noticed that the trees and gardens were even larger and more colorful than in Los Angeles, and that the population was more dark skinned, including many more Africans and East Indians than in my time. I remarked on this to OB.

"Yes," he said, "the proportion of Japanese and Chinese in the local population has declined since your time, but the proportion of persons from Africa, India, and South America has markedly increased. The WFU has been careful to recruit its staff from all the nations of the world in proportion to their representation in the world intelligentsia. During its first two centuries it was dominated by advanced European countries, but today it is more democratic and strives continuously to demonstrate this fact by hiring employees from all member nations in proportion to their supplies of skilled and professional workers."

8. The WFU Parliament

By now we had crossed the greenbelt surrounding the city center and entered the center itself. OB began to name the principal buildings, all surrounded by gardens and trees, as we passed them--the luxury department store, the medical complex, the auditorium, the art museum, the stadium, the hotel, etc. The only building I recognized was the original royal Hawaiian palace, often seen on TV in my time, which had either been beautifully preserved or reconstructed. Across the street from it was a large handsome building housing the WFU Parliament and offices for members of this body, and their staffs. We turned into the basement garage of this building, parked our car, and proceeded to the gallery of the Parliament meeting hall where the Parliament was in session. After we were seated, I began to question OB about it.

"I assume that this is a one-chamber legislature, like the U.S. Congress," I said. "How many members does it have, and how are they chosen?"

"It has 120 members who serve overlapping six year terms. They are selected by the legislatures of the countries they reprsent, from the senior members of those legislatures. Thus all have had long professional training in social science and much experience in legislation. As you may have already been told, we strongly believe in government by experts."

"And who selects the chief executive of the WFU?" I enquired.

"He or she is selected by the WFU Parliament from among the senior professional executives of the world government."

At this point I shifted my attention to the action on the floor of the Parliament Chamber and observed that a handsome brown-skinned gentleman was addressing a sparsely occupied chamber. "Who is he and what is he talking about?" I asked.

"He is one of the eight delegates from North India, and he is opposing certain proposed changes in Voca. All final decisions concerning the continuous reform of Voca are made by the WFU because all the peoples of the world use Voca. No individual nation is allowed to change their language because this would make international communication more difficults. The WFU devotes nearly all of its time and funds to the solution of such international and world-wide problems, leaving the solution of purely national problems to the national governments."

"But are members of a legislature competent to decide on details of language reform?" I enquired. "I thought you practiced government by experts."

"We practice government by experts whenever and wherever it does not arouse excessive popular protest. Language reform is one of the few public policies which arouses wide public interest and, occasionally, strong public protest. The function of all legislatures today is to give the public a sense of control over those policies in which most people are deeply interested. But the vast majority of political issues arouse little if any public interest, and can therefore be handled by experts. Of course, you must bear in mind that our experts are far more competent, and therefore far more respected than your own."

While I was pondering this answer, the Parliament adjourned. OB led me out of the gallery and guided me through a tour of the public areas of the

Parliament Building, including a library, a museum, and an empty committee room. At the conclusion of our tour, he made a telephone call at a public telephone, and turned to me with a happy expression on his face.

"I have just confirmed that B9, the Chief Executive of the WFU, would like to have us lunch with her in her private residence. I did not tell you in advance of this invitation because it was not definite, and I did not want to disappoint you. But I have just talked to her secretary, and he informed me that she is expecting us for lunch in half an hour. The lunch will be at her home because the authorities are still keeping your revival and existence a secret."

9. Lunch with the WFU Chief Executive

We visited the nearest public rest room to groom ourselves for this important visit, and then took an elevator to the basement garage where we had left our cart. We did a few minutes sightseeing, and then drove straight to her residence which turned out to be a single-family house little if any larger than the one in which I had been reared. I could not help commenting on this fact as we parked before it.

"Yes, it is very small compared with your White House," OB concluded. "But that is just another evidence of the far more equal income distribution prevailing today. The salary of this chief executive is only twice the average wage level. She would have to spend a third of her income to hire a single full-time house servant, and probably has only one part-time servant. Of course, she does not have to pay for the policeman by the door, and has the free use of elaborate offices and reception rooms."

We were admitted by a young girl, presumably the part-time maid, and ushered into a modest but comfortable living room. The Chief Executive, a large and imposing mulatto, rose to greet us as we entered, and conducted us almost immediately to a small living room. I could see that she was studying me very carefully, as if I were a strange animal in a zoo, which of course I almost was.

As soon as we were seated, she began to ask about such details as my age, birthplace, occupation, etc. Fortunately, OB was able to answer many of these questions quickly and briefly without bothering me. Then B9 paused, looked at me, and asked, "What has pleased you the most about our new world?"

"It is the creation of a world government, and the resulting world peace and order which has pleased me the most," I replied. "In my time most intelligent people feared that the world would be repeatedly devastated and depopulated by nuclear wars. We knew that it was possible to create a peaceful and prosperous world order, but most national leaders were willing to destroy the world in order to preserve national honor, prestige, or a specific economic system. My country's favorite motto was, "Better dead than red," which meant that they preferred death to rule by communists, and the later phrase was very broadly defined. Of course, the Russian communist leaders were equally opposed to rational compromise and peaceful co-existence. So it seems wonderful, and almost incredible, that you have long enjoyed world government and world peace."

At this time the part-time maid announced that lunch was ready, and the three of us adjourned to the dining room, where most of the food was already on the table. I was greatly impressed by the simplicity and informality of hospitality in the private residence of the first woman of the world. How vastly more elaborate and luxurious it would have been in my time!

When we were seated, I began the conversation as follows: "My guide and mentor has informed me that you are a native of South Africa, which seemed about to endure a bitter civil war in my last days. I am curious to know how the political conflict was solved."

"What years are you speaking of?"

"The 1980's," I said.

After a moment's thought, she replied, "Yes, I remember, that was indeed a difficult period in our history. The bitter conflict continued for several decades after your time, but one concession after another was granted the blacks, until about 2020, when the blacks finally achieved political domination and ended all racial discrimination. Some whites left the country, but the great majority remained in the country and gradually merged with the native population. Like nearly all South Africans today, I have English, German, and Dutch ancestors, as well as negro ancestors."

"What language became dominant in South Africa after the liberation?" I enquired.

"The new black rulers chose English, both because it was the leading international language of Africa and because they considered Africaans the

language of their major oppressors. But today of
course we all speak Voca."
     After this the Chief Executive expertly resumed
her questioning of me and I told her a great deal
about my life and my era, which I need not repeat
here. I was gratified by her keen interest and
astonished by her wide knowledge of my era. We knew
that she was a busy executive, and more than once
suggested that we ought to leave, but she kept us for
an hour after lunch and explained finally that only a
very important engagement made it necessary for her
to leave us.
     OB and I returned to our electric cart and spent
another hour touring the city before ending up at the
bus depot where we turned in our rented cart and took
an express bus to the airport. Once on the plane, I
meditated for some time on my incredible experience.
As our plane rose from the airport, I had a fine view
of Pearl Harbor, which contained several airplane
carriers and nuclear armed submarines. I watched the
beautiful green Hawaiian Islands as long as they were
visible and then turned to address my companion.

                    10. On Futurism

     "How I wish I could return to my own era and
people and tell them how much I have learned from you
and your age!" I exclaimed. "I could have shown them
how to avoid a vast amount of human sorrow and suffering."
     "You are being quite irrational," OB replied.
"The past is gone and cannot be revisited. Moreover,
even if you could return, you could tell them little
that was new to them. The science of futurism had
already begun to develop rapidly in your time, and
continued to do so after you were frozen. Within a
decade after your departure, futurists had predicted
all the major long-run social trends which would
characterize the history of the next five hundred
years. In fact a brilliant book, The Next 500 Years,
was published in (1967), some time before you were
frozen. If you had read it, you would have found
little to surprise you in our society."
     "I never heard of it," I said. "Why did it
receive so little attention?"
     "In your time most new social theories were un-
popular and neglected when first stated. And, during
the cold war, theories of radical social change were
especially unpopular in America, but sound social
theories always survive and receive more and more

acceptance in an advanced society like the U.S. in 1980. Within a few decades, the many sound predictions stated in this and other later futurist books were generally accepted by American social scientists.

11. On Future Progress

As our plane flew almost silently through the night, I mentally reviewed all of the almost incredible facts I had been told about the prosperous, healthy, and peaceful new world around me. Surely there must be some flaws in it that had escaped me. Then it occurred to me that people living in such a world might have little hope of future social progress and scientific discovery. I decided to raise this point with OB.

"In my time," I remarked, "intelligent people in every country were full of hope for great and exciting social and scientific progress in the future. Millions of our best citizens devoted their lives to social reform and scientific research. Each had a serious purpose in life, and therefore found life profoundly meaningful and satisfying. Now that you have achieved all the progress they dreamed of, and much that they had not even conceived of, life for such people must seem relatively dull and purposeless. Do you have any great social reforms or important or exciting research projects under way?"

"We have found," OB replied, "that the solution, usually only a partial solution, of one social or scientific problem nearly always creates or reveals new problems. Human demand for social and scientific progress is as insatiable as human demand for economic goods and services. We are studying more challenging and exciting problems than you faced in your time."

"I cannot imagine them," I said. "Could you give me some examples?"

"Certainly," OB replied. "Let me begin with problems of language. I believe you have been told that the creation and general use of our new language, Voca, made it possible for everyone to think more rapidly and clearly. We now believe that much further progress in this direction is possible. Several promising language research projects are under way, and we are confident that future language reforms will markedly improve the ability of people to reason clearly, write faster, read more easily, and use typewriters and computers more effectively.

"Secondly, we are conducting numerous very

-184-

promising research projects on human eugenic improvement. We believe we will soon be able to eliminate or minimize several more major hereditary causes of mental illness, and many more causes of minor unhappiness.

"Thirdly, we are seriously considering the arguments for and against a human breeding program which would reduce the average weight of human beings by 50%. Such a program would enable us to double the population of the earth, or to double the per capita consumption of tangible economic goods, without increasing the strain upon our natural resources. This is the kind of problem which is suitable for solution by public opinion polls and requires little scientific research. We know how to alter human size within wide limits. But there are strong emotions about proposals to reduce the size of the average person.

"Fourth, we are engaged in elaborate and expensive efforts to communicate with rational beings in other solar systems. These are the most important and exciting of all our contemporary scientific research projects. Contact with such beings would yield fascinating information, and also create great social problems. And we believe such contact is inevitable because there are millions of planets where rational beings can exist.

"Fifth, although we have made great improvements in our schools since your day, we are still conducting major experiments in educational methods. Some of these are very promising. We are confident that we can make education much more interesting to students and much more productive in results. Of course, we now concentrate on research in adult education because such education continues for many more years than pre-adult education.

"Finally, millions of artists and writers find life highly satisfying and purposeful because they are striving to create new and/or more beautiful or exciting works of art—paintings, building plans, novels, dramas, gardens, etc. Moreover, the proportion of our population which is both capable of creating great works of art and has time to do so is far higher than in your era."

12. On Space Colonization

"In my day," I commented, "many people dreamed of colonizing space, the moon, other planets of our solar system, and even more remote planets. Why don't your contemporaries have such plans?"

"Since your time, the progress of applied science has created, and is still creating, so many and so promising opportunities for profitable investment and colonization on Earth that we doubt it will ever be possible to make more profitable investments in space colonies. Almost every scientific discovery which reduces the cost of space travel and colonization reduces equally or more the cost of colonizing infertile and inhospitable regions on Earth. And the least hospitable of these regions, for instance, the North and South Pole areas, are much more suitable for human settlement than Mars or the Moon, the most promising areas for space settlement. We have not yet colonized the polar regions, but we have colonized most of the desert and mountainous areas on Earth, and we have greatly enlarged and improved more fertile areas all over the Earth. In sum, we have always found it more economic to improve and/or colonize the least fertile regions on Earth than to colonize space, and we expect no change in this policy in the foreseeable future."

"But couldn't you obtain vast quantities of scarce and valuable minerals from the Moon, the planets, meteorites, and other objects in space?" I enquired.

"Yes, we could, but we can always obtain them more cheaply by digging deeper in the Earth or by processing ocean water. Your contemporaries were correct in predicting that space travel, exploration, colonization, and mining would become ever cheaper and more feasible. But they were almost entirely wrong in predicting that such activities would become more profitable than such activities on Earth. It is far cheaper to level a mountain on the Earth and colonize the new level area than to create a similar colony on the Moon or in Space."

13. A Vivid Nightmare

By this time I was beginning to feel tired and sleepy. I relaxed in my comfortable lounge chair, listened to the gentle hum of the airplane motors, and soon fell asleep. I dreamed that I was taking a walk on Main Street in old Los Angeles. I saw homeless men sleeping in doorways, passed garishly dressed teen-age prostitutes, saw the glaring advertisements of pornographic theaters, breathed the toxic fumes emitted by passing cars, and passed numerous saloons, liquor stores, gun shops, and cheap jewelry

and clothing stores. In disgust, I moved on to a
high-fashion shopping area, where shop windows displayed the latest styles of luxury goods designed to
promote conspicuous consumption and rapid obsolescence. I stopped before a store selling expensive
TV sets to listen to a heated debate on foreign
policy. I heard a famous Senator warn us of terrible
danger from an evil empire bent on conquering and
ruling America. We must redouble our efforts to prepare for a nuclear war, he proclaimed. When his
opponent spoke of the vast destruction a nuclear war
would cause, he boldly asserted that it is far better
to be dead than red. I was so irritated by this
offer to sacrifice my life and property for his
fanatic purpose that I could not refrain from reply-
ing, as if he were present, "No! No! No! I want to
live. Life is better than death. As long as we have
life we have hope." At least that is what I meant to
reply. In fact, I could not open my mouth. I became
quite excited and struggled more and more vigorously
to express myself. Then I felt someone tugging
vigorously at my right arm, and suddenly I awoke. OB
was pulling my arm and was saying, "Wake up, wake up.
You are having a bad dream."
      Slowly I came to myself. It had indeed been a
horrible nightmare, not an awakening from a utopian
dream! I felt myself and the objects around me to be
sure I was awake. I thanked OB, and told him what I
had dreamed. Above all, I felt a wonderful glow of
intense relief and pleasure that I really was living
in a new world so greatly superior to the one I had
come from, so vividly remembered in my nightmare!
And again I felt an intense desire to learn more and
more about my new world and how it had been created.
The thought that I could go on living in this exciting new world and learning ever more about it gave me
profound satisfaction. Surely I was the most fortunate of men, the first of all men to live in two
different ages and study the differences between.
them. In this happy mood I relaxed and looked for-
ward with vast contentment to my continued study of
life in the 25th century. I looked out of my window
and saw the morning sun rising over California in a
clear smog-free air. Surely it was a significant
omen of my bright and stimulating future!

ABOUT THE AUTHOR

Born in Carthage, Missouri, in 1904, and raised largely in Pasadena, California, Burnham Putnam Beckwith was graduated from Stanford University with a B.A. in Philosophy in 1926. He spent the next two years at the Harvard Business School, and, after three more years of full-time graduate study, received a Ph.D. in economics from the University of Southern California in 1932. He held a post-doctoral research-training assistanship under Dr. Edward L. Thorndike at Teachers' College, Columbia University, from 1935 to 1937. He also taught economics at the University of Kansas, Queens College (NYC), and the University of Georgia before going to work for the War Production Board (D.C.) in 1941. From 1945 to 1948 he worked for the War Department in France (Biarritz American University) and in Germany (OMGUS, Berlin).

Since 1948 he has been an independant researcher and author, and has published a dozen books, most of which have described coming social trends and reforms. They include The Next 500 Years, Scientific Predictions of Major Social Trends (1967); Government by Experts, The Next Stage in Political Evolution (1972); Liberal Socialism, The Welfare Economics of a Liberal Socialist Economy (1974); Free Goods, The Theory of Free or Communist Distribution (1976); and Radical Essays (1981). He has also published several recent articles in The Futurist and The World Future Society Bulletin.